MARGARET
ATWOOD

A BEGINNER'S GUIDE

MARGARET ATWOOD

A BEGINNER'S GUIDE

PILAR CUDER

Series Editors
Rob Abbott & Charlie Bell

Hodder & Stoughton

A MEMBER OF THE HODDER HEADLINE GROUP

Orders: please contact Bookpoint Ltd, 130 Milton Park, Abingdon, Oxon OX14 4SB.
Telephone: (44) 01235 827720, Fax: (44) 01235 400454. Lines are open from 9.00–6.00,
Monday to Saturday, with a 24-hour message answering service.
You can also order through our website www.madaboutbook.co.uk

British Library Cataloguing in Publication Data
A catalogue record for this title is available from The British Library

ISBN 0 340 85737 4

First published 2003
Impression number   10 9 8 7 6 5 4 3 2 1
Year 2007 2006 2005 2004 2003

Copyright © 2003 Pilar Cuder

"Portrait of the Artist as a Young Cypher" from The Thomas Fisher Rare Book Library.
Cover photo from Corbis
Typeset by Transet Limited, Coventry, England.
Printed in Great Britain for Hodder & Stoughton Educational, a division of Hodder Headline
Plc, 338 Euston Road, London NW1 3BH by Cox & Wyman, Reading, Berks.

CONTENTS

How to use this book

The *Beginner's Guide* series aims to introduce readers to major writers of the past 500 years. It is assumed that readers will begin with little or no knowledge and will want to go on to explore the subject in other ways.

BEGIN READING THE AUTHOR

This book is a companion guide to Atwood's major works; it is not a substitute for reading the books themselves. It would be useful if you read some of the works in parallel, so that you can put theory into practice. This book is divided into sections. After considering how to approach the author's work and a brief biography, we go on to explore some of Atwood's main writings and themes before examining some critical approaches to the author. The survey finishes with suggestions for further reading and possible areas of further study.

HOW TO APPROACH UNFAMILIAR OR DIFFICULT TEXTS

Coming across a new writer may seem daunting, but do not be put off. The trick is to persevere. Much good writing is multi-layered and complex. It is precisely this diversity and complexity which makes literature rewarding and exhilarating.

Literary work often needs to be read more than once and in different ways. These ways can include: a leisurely and superficial reading to get the main ideas and narrative; a slower more detailed reading focusing on the nuances of the text and on what appear to be key passages; and reading in a random way, moving back and forth through the text to examine different aspects, such as themes, narrative or characterization.

In complex texts it may be necessary to read in short chunks. When it comes to tackling difficult words or concepts it is often enough to guess in context on the first reading, making a more detailed study using a dictionary or book of critical concepts on later reading. If you prefer to look up unusual words as you go along, be careful that you do not disrupt the flow of the text and your concentration.

VOCABULARY

You will see that keywords and unfamiliar terms are set in **bold** text. These words are defined and explained in the glossary to be found at the back of the book.

This book is a tool to help you appreciate a key figure in literature. We hope you enjoy reading it and find it useful.

✳ ✳ ✳ *SUMMARY* ✳ ✳ ✳

To maximize the use of this book:

- read the author's work

- read it several times in different ways

- be open to innovative or unusual forms of writing

- persevere.

Why Read Margaret Atwood Today?

INTERNATIONAL ACCLAIM

Margaret Atwood is the best-known Canadian writer outside Canada. She is alone in her generation in having made the transition from a popular national author to wide international acclaim. She has been awarded the Governor General's Award for fiction (1985) as well as for poetry (1966) in Canada, and the Booker Prize in Britain (2000). She ranks among the best-selling authors of all times, and her success is unlikely to fade. On the contrary, these days her novels are translated into dozens of languages as soon as they are published. Like Toni Morrison and Nadine Gordimer, who also come from English-speaking communities other than Britain, she has managed to combine the appeal of local issues and landscapes with stories and characters that people across the world may sympathize with.

AN INFLUENTIAL FIGURE

Margaret Atwood is more than a writer. She is a cultural icon. She grew up in a country without a literature of its own. At school and at university, she studied British or American writers, but no Canadian literature had reached the classroom yet. She contributed to change this state of affairs both as a critic and as a publisher. In her thematic guide to Canadian literature, *Survival*, she was among the first to suggest that Canadian texts possessed truly distinctive features. Later, with the foundation of House of Anansi Press, she helped young writers reach an increasing readership. Since then, she has continued to be an influential voice in cultural politics both inside and outside her country.

SERIOUS FUN

Margaret Atwood's novels are built around a central mystery or riddle: a death, real or pretended, a strange disappearance, a murder or other act of violence. Why does Joan have to fake her death in *Lady Oracle*? Has Offred in *The Handmaid's Tale* managed to reach safety? Was Grace in *Alias Grace* really a cold-blooded murderer? Readers are led into an expanding maze of possible explanations, and at the end of the novel we are shocked or grieved or surprised by unexpected disclosures. As a result, Atwood's novels can't be put down.

But Atwood never names all the truths. Unlike conventional detective stories, there is no clear-cut answer, no identifiable culprit. There is seldom complete closure. Instead, this fiction, like real life, remains multiple and open-ended, and readers are encouraged to choose their own interpretation.

POSTMODERNISM AT ITS BEST

The key to Atwood's style lies in her unique blend of voice and memory. Typically, she chooses the voice of a woman who is troubled

KEYWORD

Postmodernism: A literary movement of the second half of the twentieth century, based on the revision of the ideas and aesthetics of modernism. Postmodernism questions the existence of universal truths and distrusts those disciplines that try to provide general answers to the problems of human life, such as History, Religion or Philosophy.

by some past event. This woman, who tends to be white, middle class and heterosexual, then leads readers little by little into a recreation of those events she lived through or otherwise knows about. Atwood's complex use of point of view tricks us into becoming more and more immersed in and intrigued by the narrator's life and troubles.

Atwood's protagonist-narrators are often artists, journalists (like Rennie in *Bodily Harm*), painters (like Elaine in *Cat's Eye*), writers (like Iris in *The Blind Assassin*), or they are otherwise creative (like Grace the accomplished quilt-maker in *Alias Grace)*. Art is the lens through which they try to make sense of things, but they are trapped into the passive stance of the viewer, detached interpreters instead of involved actors.

By bringing together fragments of their past, they construct a tale for us to interpret. The fragments themselves are not necessarily similar. Atwood likes to blend different kinds of materials and conventions in her novels. Thus, she includes letters and reports, newspaper accounts, scientific records, alongside more straightforward storytelling. She also moves from the parameters of science fiction and dystopian writing to the romantic or the Gothic from one novel to the next.

FEMINIST FOOD FOR THOUGHT

Storytelling is an essential activity for Atwood's narrators. They are women driven by the need to transmit their own and other women's stories. By telling them, they make sense of their own lives and of their relationships with other women, whether they are their ancestors (often mothers) or their contemporaries (sisters, friends). By telling them, they live on in the next generations, because their stories will become real to the intended recipients, daughters, granddaughters, women of the future.

More often than not these stories have to do with women being (ab)used by those with power over them, mostly men, but at times also other women. Rennie in *Bodily Harm* lives in panic after an anonymous stalker breaks into her house. Laura in *The Blind Assassin* suffers child abuse and is locked into a mental institution. These are only two examples of the violence against women that Margaret Atwood denounces in her writing.

A CHALLENGING WORLD VIEW

By weaving stories and points of view, Margaret Atwood successfully challenges one-sided world views. In her writing, objectivity is always deceptive, a mere pretence. A façade that may hide more obscure interests. Simon Jordan in *Alias Grace* hides behind the smoke screen of scientific discourse, pretending to be in control of his life and his body when he is in fact troubled by volcanic passions.

For Atwood, perspective is all in the onlooker's eye, and perceptions are necessarily subjective and partial. No two accounts will ever be exactly the same, and therefore no one can make a rightful claim to History. Objective historicity is replaced in her work by relativism, the best case in point being the different accounts of Zenia's character in *The Robber Bride*. There are always more sides to a story than we may at first expect.

✳ ✳ ✳ *SUMMARY* ✳ ✳ ✳

We should read Atwood today because:

● she is one of the major women writers of her generation, and her work has won wide international recognition

● she is an influential figure, a spokesperson for many current cultural concerns

● she pulls us into fictional worlds with her masterful use of suspense and mystery

● the postmodern techniques in her writing constitute a rewarding challenge to readers

● she writes women's stories and makes us think about women's lives

● she satirizes narrow truths and emphasizes pluralism.

How to Approach Margaret Atwood's Work

Margaret Atwood's writing, whether poetry or prose, is usually good fun. In fact, it is so easy to read that you may at first wonder at its simplicity of style. Once you examine it in detail, however, you will find that such simplicity is the result of a very careful choice of words, and a complex arrangement of ideas, characters and events. As an illustration of this deceptive simplicity, let us consider one of Atwood's early poems, 'At the tourist centre in Boston'. Here we will find already many of the key features of Atwood's style.

'AT THE TOURIST CENTRE IN BOSTON'

Atwood wrote this poem in the 1960s, when she was studying in Boston. In it, the speaker tries to look at her own country with the eyes of a foreigner. Facing a map of Canada and ten photographs (one for each Canadian province), she describes with detachment what she can see: dots and names for the cities, mountains and lakes for the land. Atwood's choice of words makes clear that these images of Canada are too neat to be truthful. The rocks are conveniently arranged, the blues of the lakes are too pure, the camp fire does not smoke, the place looks uninhabited. The apparent objectivity of the map and the pictures seems inadequate for the speaker. At the end of the section, she wonders 'whose dream is this?'

Next, Atwood contrasts the coldly clean image of the tourist centre with her own reminiscences of Canada. The idea of purity and emptiness is challenged in this second section. In her memories there were people, machines, garbage, slush. We have to wonder who is wrong, which Canada is the real one. Will she return to find that everything has changed? Has she dreamed it all? The poem ends on a note of uncertainty, with the puzzled question, 'Who really lives there?' As usual, Atwood prefers to leave her writing open-ended, and steers clear of a neat, closed ending. Instead, she is asking her readers to take sides, to come up with answers to the questions she raises.

Atwood tackles here several important issues. First, the unequal relation between the United States and Canada. In the poem, Americans are shown as the consumers and Canadians as the consumed. Grinning tourists take possession of the forests, the trails, the mountains, while the citizens go missing. Canada appears to be open to conquest. It is a very unsettling idea, at least for a Canadian. In the 1960s, Canadians felt uncertain about their own identity, and this often took the shape of a feeling of inferiority to Americans, who were much more assertive and self-confident (or so Canadians thought).

Second, the poet deals with the related issues of perception, representation and interpretation. Like the speaker's, our gaze is directed to the map and the photos. We are required to ponder their meaning. Obviously, reducing such a large country to just ten photos implies a simplification of the object represented. What's more, oversimplifying and sanitizing Canada may have a further motive, that the poem defines as 'a lure for export'. Although at first we might believe that the contours of the map and the machine-made photos are reliable pieces of information, the poem denies their objectivity. Instead, here they have become instruments of deception, inducing dreams, fantasies, hallucinations. By such means, the poet is hinting at the politics of representation, at the fact that there may be a hidden purpose to all forms of representation. The person in control of the production and distribution of an image necessarily defines the object according to his or her own interests, whether this is a conscious process or not.

The poem ends with a question, 'Who really lives there?' This is not by chance, nor is it a sign of stylistic carelessness. On the contrary, in this key location the question works as a bridge between the speaker/poet and her readers, and it is meant to pass on the burden of interpretation to us. This is fairly typical of Atwood's works. For this writer, no one can or should remain indifferent. Everything is political, and everyone has to decide whose side they are on.

These comments can be applied to Atwood's fiction as well. A case in point is her short story 'Happy Endings', from her collection of short prose *Murder in the Dark* (1983).

'HAPPY ENDINGS'

Atwood wrote this short story approximately one decade after the poem 'At the tourist centre in Boston'. It is a remarkable example of **metafiction**, and as such it is very representative of Atwood's ideas about storytelling and its function in contemporary society. The story starts with a riddle: 'John and

KEYWORD

Metafiction: Self-conscious fiction. A story that discusses the how and why of writing fiction, and their implications.

Mary meet. What happens then?' The several possible plots deriving from this initial meeting are described and classified under labels A to F, and followed by some authorial comments.

'A' follows the conventional lives of John and Mary. They get married and have children, a nice house, good jobs. They die, contented, of old age.

'B' is an unhappy love story. Mary feels used by an unloving John. It is a long, miserable relationship. When she finds out that John is seeing another woman, she commits suicide. John then marries the other woman, and at this point 'B' becomes the plot in 'A', with John and his wife living conventionally happy lives to their deaths.

'C' unravels another unhappy love story, this time between a younger, unloving Mary and an older, married John. When he finds her in bed with a younger man, he shoots them and himself. His widow then marries another man, and the story again becomes 'A'.

In 'D', relationships don't matter. Instead, the couple has to face a disaster, a tidal wave that destroys their charming house on the beach and kills thousands. Then 'D' once more merges into 'A'.

'E' has the man suffer a long disease and the woman patiently nurse him until he dies. Then she lives on until her uneventful death, as in 'A'.

In 'F', the author suggests that, for more complication, John should be made into a revolutionary and Mary into a counterespionage agent. After a while, this plot will become 'A' too.

The author's comments at the end of the story help us understand the story and put the several plots in perspective. She explains that the only true ending is death: 'John and Mary die'. Although this may seem shocking at first, we must admit that it is at the same time obvious. All stories deal with human life, which boils down to the biological facts of birth (beginning), reproduction (middle) and death (end). Similarly, falling in love, getting married, being ill, etc., are on the whole unremarkable ingredients of anyone's life. In that sense, we may agree with the author that events in themselves are not enough to build an interesting story. Instead, we are asked to consider that what matters is the 'how' and the 'why'. These are the elements that make each human life unique, and therefore each story different, a world complete in itself.

Once more, Atwood insists that we look beyond the basic components of writing. Literature is not merely a matter of putting several ready-made ingredients together. Style is important, but should not be overestimated. Rather, we should try to consider the less apparent elements. Reading this story, we establish a certain complicity with the author. Atwood has laid bare the process of writing, and she has made us aware of the choices writers have, and of the implications of these choices.

Margaret Atwood makes it possible for readers to co-operate in the production of meaning. In all of her writing, whether prose or verse, we are meant to participate actively in the process of reading, and not just to accept whatever an all-powerful author would like us to believe.

✳ ✳ ✳ SUMMARY ✳ ✳ ✳

● Maps, photos, and in general all surfaces and images, are usually deceptive in Atwood's writing.

● Readers are expected to look beyond surfaces and to consider the politics of representation.

● In Atwood's writing, readers are expected to participate actively and not just to behave as passive observers.

3 Biography and Influences

IN THE BUSH

Margaret Eleanor Atwood was born in Ottawa in 1939. Her parents came originally from Nova Scotia, the descendants of New England Loyalists who had settled there in the eighteenth century, after the American Independence. She has a brother and a sister. Her father was a zoologist, and he conducted his research in the woods when he was not teaching. So, although Margaret Atwood lived in the city during the winter months, she also spent long periods in the woods of northern Ontario and Quebec. As a result of these childhood experiences, Atwood developed a long-lasting interest in landscape and in the wilderness, which often surfaces in her writing in her characters' mixed feelings towards nature, appeal but also fear, familiarity as well as total estrangement.

TORONTO AND BOSTON

When she was seven, Margaret Atwood's family moved to Toronto, the city that has become her home. Although she has lived in many cities all over the world (Boston, Vancouver, Berlin, Edinburgh among others), she always returns to Toronto, and the city is often remarkably present in her novels. There she attended school and high school. In those days, Canada was still in many ways a British colony. The official flag was Britain's Union Jack and students started their day singing 'God save the King', as Atwood herself would later describe in *Cat's Eye*. The emblems and symbols that we identify with Canada nowadays had not yet come into being. The maple leaf was adopted as the national flag in 1965, and '*Oh Canada!*' would become the national anthem in 1980.

In 1957 she went on to take a degree in English at Victoria College of the University of Toronto. This was an exciting place to be in at the time, especially because of the presence of a first-rate intellectual,

Northrop Frye, who represented the **archetypal school of criticism**. There Atwood also met other writers of her generation, such as Dennis Lee, and of the previous one, such as the poet Jay Macpherson, who taught Victorian Literature at Victoria College. By now Atwood had started to write poetry, and she regularly contributed to the university newsletter and magazine. She wrote and printed her first poetry collection in 1961, *Double Persephone*, which won the E.J. Pratt Medal.

KEYWORD

Archetypal criticism: School of literary criticism, prominent in the 1950s and 1960s, which identified the repeated presence of certain myths and archetypes in world literature through the ages. The most representative text is Northrop Frye's *Anatomy of Criticism* (1957).

This is how Atwood has pictured herself as a student and a young writer at the University of Toronto in the late 1950's.

The same year, Atwood went to Harvard to pursue graduate work in English Literature. There she continued to develop her interest in the Gothic and the Victorians and took several courses on American Literature taught by Perry Miller, to whom she would later dedicate her novel *The Handmaid's Tale* (1985).

NATIONAL RECOGNITION

Between 1965 and 1985, Margaret Atwood's creative work gained national recognition. She first became known for her poetry. Her second collection of poetry, *The Circle Game*, published by a very small press, managed to win the most prestigious national award in 1966, the Governor General's Award for Poetry in English. Larger Canadian publishers declared their interest in the young poet, and *The Circle Game* was soon followed by other chapbooks – *The Animals in That Country* (1968), *The Journals of Susanna Moodie* (1970), *Procedures for Underground* (1970) – as well as by two novels, *The Edible Woman* (1969) and *Surfacing* (1972), all of which met with popular as well as critical approval.

During this period, Atwood's engagement with Canadian literature and culture grew to be very active. She joined the board of House of Anansi Press, a new publishing company started by Dennis Lee which sought to publish and promote Canadian works. She also put some of her thoughts on Canadian Literature into a critical study, *Survival* (1972). Atwood designed this book as a basic tool for the teaching of Canadian Literature, which was then picking up in some Canadian universities. She recommended readings and included useful sections on resources, since this was a time when many libraries and bookshops did not carry Canadian books. Following Frye, who believed that some myths were ever present in all world literature of whatever period, Atwood's main thesis was that 'every country or culture has a single unifying and informing symbol at its core' (*Survival: A Thematic Guide to Canadian Literature.* Toronto: House of Anansi Press, 1972, p. 31). Examples of this kind of symbol are the frontier in American literature and the island in English literature. Atwood argues that survival is the Canadian symbol, because many works, past and present, have to do with the struggle to survive in a new and often hostile land. Often, survival is not possible, and endings tend to be rather gloomy. As a result, Atwood concludes that Canadians (as a country, as individuals, and in their literature) exhibit the pessimistic attitude of victims. Finally, she establishes four basic victim positions, ranging from complete denial of one's actual victimization to liberation from such a role.

Survival caused a stir in Canadian circles. Its approach was considered valid by many, especially because it was congenial to the ends of Canadian nationalism. Others turned to the search for an analysis of relevant themes in Canadian literature, thus contributing to the rise of **thematic criticism**. However, it was attacked by many who failed to see the book for what it was, a valuable starting point for the study of a literature that few had cared for in

KEYWORD

Thematic criticism: School of literary criticism, prominent in Canada in the 1970s and 1980s, which discussed the unifying presence of certain themes in Canadian literature, especially those related to the land and nature.

the past. Instead, they took Atwood's proposals as articles of faith, and accused her of dogmatism. Nowadays, thematic criticism by itself cannot explain the variety of Canadian literature, and many of its theses have been challenged because too often they betray the point of view of the white settler. Yet, many critics continue to find Atwood's thoughts on victimization useful to explain her own writing, and especially her women characters.

Atwood's participation in the cultural struggles of this period made her very visible, and she was the target of some virulent attacks, some of them very painful because they attacked her not just as a writer, but as a woman writer. After a first failed marriage with the American scholar and editor James Polk, Margaret Atwood started a new relationship with the writer Graeme Gibson. They left Toronto for the quiet of the countryside, and for several years they lived on a farm in Alliston, Ontario. Their daughter Jess was born in 1976.

Nevertheless, Margaret Atwood's output in the next few years was steady. She produced three more novels: *Lady Oracle* (1976), *Life Before Man* (1979) and *Bodily Harm* (1981). Nor did she stop writing poetry and short stories. She lectured and read from her works both in Canada and abroad, and reviewed the work of other authors. She also continued to intervene in the cultural arena. She participated in the creation of the Writer's Union of Canada, which she presided in 1981–82, and gave her support to another association of writers, PEN Canada, later serving as its President. The literary journal *The Malahat Review* devoted a special issue to her in 1977. Atwood had attained national recognition.

INTERNATIONAL FAME

Margaret Atwood's next breakthrough came in 1985, with the publication of her novel *The Handmaid's Tale*, which was nominated for the Booker Prize. The novel was and is tremendously popular. It was translated into dozens of languages, and has run through many editions. It is also her only novel to have become a film so far, with a script by Harold Pinter, starring Natasha Richardson under the direction of Volker Schlondörff.

Although *The Handmaid's Tale* did not win the Booker Prize, it was awarded the Commonwealth Prize, confirming Atwood's international celebrity, as well as bringing her a second Governor General's Award, this time for fiction. Her remaining four novels have all been well received by readers and critics alike, and have brought Atwood a string of nominations and awards. Her next novels, *Cat's Eye* (1988) and *Alias Grace* (1996) were again shortlisted for the Booker Prize, which she finally won in 2000 for *The Blind Assassin. The Robber Bride* (1993) obtained again the Commonwealth Prize, and *Alias Grace* the very prestigious Giller Prize.

Besides the novels, Atwood has published more poetry and short stories, critical pieces and lectures. Her involvement in political issues, such as environmental and human rights, continues to this date. Together with Toni Morrison and Nadine Gordimer (both of them Nobel Prize winners), nowadays Margaret Atwood is no doubt the best-known and most widely read woman author in English, as well as the most international of English-Canadian writers.

✳ ✳ ✳ *SUMMARY* ✳ ✳ ✳

In looking at Margaret Atwood's life we can see that:

• her writing was marked by her early visits to the Canadian bush

• she struggled to find a tradition of Canadian literature that she felt deprived of

• she has always been committed to the development of Canadian literature and culture

• she supports human and environmental rights.

4 Major Themes

Margaret Atwood's novels have many layers of meanings. Although it is not easy to summarize their main features, here are some keys that will help you understand them better.

THE GOTHIC

At the bottom of each Atwoodian plot lies a mystery, often in the shape of a corpse. Most of her narrators are obsessed with some past event that returns to haunt them. Death, whether real or staged, violent or natural, accidental or not, but never completely explained, is hardly ever absent from her fiction and it exerts its fascination over readers and author alike. Atwood masterfully uses mystery to hook readers into turning the book pages. For instance, *Lady Oracle* (1976) starts with the stunning statement: 'I planned my death carefully' (ch. 1). Although we soon learn that what the narrator planned was a fake death, and not her actual suicide, the event in itself is so extraordinary that we are eager to find out more about the motivations of this character. Similarly, the strange circumstances surrounding the accidental death of Laura in *The Blind Assassin* (2000) pose a challenge that makes us search for clues in the unfolding narrative of her sister, Iris Chase.

Gothic settings

Atwood's debt to the Gothic tradition is evident in the settings she chooses for these mysteries, particularly in her characters' vague sensations of danger, no matter whether they are indoors or outdoors. If they are inside a building, they feel claustrophobic; if outside in the open, they feel exposed; and in both cases, unsafe. At times Atwood uses the wilderness as the backdrop for her plot, like in *Surfacing* (1972). Then Nature turns menacing and hostile, hiding from view unspeakable threats, presences 'just behind the green leafscreen' (ch. 9). Lakes are often suspect, in part because of the likelihood of accidents, but also because of what they may hide underwater despite their calm surfaces. The narrator's brother nearly drowned in *Surfacing*; Joan fakes a boating accident in Lake Ontario (*Lady Oracle*); the three friends in *The Robber Bride* throw Zenia's ashes into those waters too.

The claustrophobic nature of some buildings in Atwood's fiction sometimes derives from the function they fulfil. For example, Grace Marks in *Alias Grace* (1996) spends most of her life in several prisons and in an asylum, where her movements are very restricted and she completely lacks privacy. However, in Atwood's use of the Gothic the familiar tends to became unfamiliar, and even a home, with its connotations of shelter and protection, can turn into a prison. In *The Handmaid's Tale* (1985), Offred's imprisonment is not enforced through locks, thick walls or heavy doors. In fact, neither her room nor the bathroom can be locked, which makes her fear someone breaking in. But Offred is confined to a handful of locations, and her movements are under constant surveillance, even in the most private places.

Finding the clues

The clues to solve the mystery are also hidden from view, and they need to be pieced together and decoded. More often than not, they are manuscripts and inscriptions tucked away in old trunks and cupboards, in the best Gothic tradition. Offred in *The Handmaid's Tale* finds in her wardrobe the mock-Latin inscription *Nolite te bastardes carborundorum* ('Don't let the bastards grind you down') left by the previous handmaid, and this message of resistance leads her on a journey of liberation. In *The Blind Assassin*, Iris keeps her diaries and heirlooms in a trunk, which she hopes her estranged granddaughter will receive after her death, thus transmitting her version of a traumatic family history, and especially the truth about her sister and herself. Likewise, cellars and attics are valuable hideouts. The Chase sisters use the attic of their family mansion to conceal Alex Thomas from the authorities (*The Blind Assassin*); Grace shares the attic with her friend Mary Whitney until she dies, and Nancy's murdered body is found in the cellar (*Alias Grace*).

Yet, Atwood also likes to play with the readers' expectations of the Gothic. Joan (*Lady Oracle*) keeps her manuscripts hidden in her underwear drawer, because she considers it the safest place. Simon Jordan tries to find out whether Grace is guilty of Nancy's and Mr Kinnear's murder by bringing her a root or a vegetable, in the hope of awakening mental associations with the cellar, and hence indirectly with the murder. Ironically, Grace's sensible, down-to-earth attitude defeats his purpose again and again, turning the tables on the doctor-patient relationship:

> 'What [Dr. Jordan] has put on the table today is a potato, but he has not yet asked me [Grace] about it, so it is just sitting there between us. I don't know what he expects me to say about it, except that I have peeled a good many of them in my time, and eaten them too, a fresh potato is a joy with a little butter and salt, and parsley if available … Sometimes I think that Dr. Jordan is a little off the head. But I would rather talk with him about potatoes, if that is what he fancies, than not talk to him at all.'
>
> (*Alias Grace*, ch. 12)

Gothic villains

Behind these mysteries there is usually a male villain, holding the strings of other people's lives. This is another recurrent feature of Gothic fiction, where the young heroine has to flee for her life from the dark, violent villain. In Atwood's novels, men have power over women and they are not afraid to use it. Joan Foster lives in permanent fear of an unidentified male figure that haunts her under many guises: the Daffodil Man of her childhood, her lover the Royal Porcupine, her husband Arthur, etc. (*Lady Oracle*). These men are ambiguous characters, sometimes perceived as rescuers, sometimes as potential killers, precisely because of the power they wield over the women. They are often endowed with great authority. They are surgeons, commanders, rich industrialists, or simply (with typical Atwoodian irony) fathers. However, they are only threatening as long as the women choose to remain passive victims. Once they realize that they are granting the men their power, the women can be free. In *The Edible Woman*, Marian lets her fiancé Peter mould her into the perfect submissive partner until she realizes that she should be the only one in charge of her own life, and breaks the engagement. In *The Blind Assassin*, Iris submits to her husband Richard Griffin for a long time. She feels it is her duty not just to him but also to her father, who had promoted the marriage in order to protect his two daughters from poverty. Her passivity proves destructive not just for her, but, even more importantly, for her younger sister Laura, who is harassed and sexually abused. Only with the death of Laura is Iris finally able to wake up from this annihilating passivity, and then she successfully confronts Richard.

WOMEN'S STORIES, WOMEN'S BODIES

Laura and Iris are not the only women to suffer oppression and bondage in Atwood's fiction. On the contrary, her stories often deal with women's issues, past and present. The main mystery (a murder, a disappearance, some unusual event) is only the tip of the iceberg, and as the narrative unfolds, other silenced stories are uncovered. Women are shown in their powerlessness, in their marginality, in their pathos, but also in their willingness to survive no matter what. In *Alias Grace*, Atwood handles the nineteenth-century story of Grace in such a way that readers can simultaneously learn about the circumstances of many other women, sometimes minor characters. We discover Grace's mother's life in Ireland, her long days of toil and childbearing, her poverty and resilience under the blows of her drunken husband, only to die while in passage to the New World. We read about Mary Whitney, the servant girl who dreams of a better life in the attic she shares with Grace and is seduced by her young master. We witness her despair as she finds out she is pregnant, and how she bleeds to death as a result of an unprofessional abortion. Next we encounter Nancy Montgomery, who lives with Thomas Kinnear as his housekeeper, but who is in fact his lover. Luckier than Mary, she has survived an abortion, but a second pregnancy has placed her in a dangerous situation, and she fears her lover will abandon her for another woman.

These stories are amplified through their common features with other stories. For instance, Dr. Jordan's landlady feels she is on the brink of disaster when her lover (who had posed as her husband) deserts her. Unprotected, she clings to an appearance of propriety while at the same time she realizes in despair that she is only steps away from a life of prostitution. All these tragic stories, encompassing several generations and social classes, come alive through Grace's voice. They are also collected in the patchwork quilts she endlessly sews, which thus become a symbol of collective suffering.

Pain and suffering

Learning to understand that pain and suffering have always been women's common lot empowers Atwood's characters and enables them to go on living. Many of them are troubled by traumatic events and experiences, and in order to overcome them they need to come to terms with their relationship to other women, especially but not exclusively their mothers. In *Surfacing*, the narrator is disappointed in her mother when she dies, and keeps expecting some message from her. In *The Handmaid's Tale*, Offred realizes too late that she should have paid more attention to her mother's warnings, and feels guilty that she resented them. In *Lady Oracle*, Joan is literally haunted by her mother's ghost, and is only rid of it when she understands that her mother too was a victim, trapped in a loveless marriage. In *Bodily Harm* (1982), Rennie learns to let go of her own pain when she is confronted by Lora's.

Repeatedly, these experiences have to do with physical trauma. Women's bodies are foregrounded in Atwood's tales. They have become alien to their owners due to society's pressure to define normal or deviant femininity, as Offred feels in *The Handmaid's Tale*, or by an acceptance to enter into a contract that makes of women sacrificial victims, like Iris in *The Blind Assassin*. Or they have turned unreliable by hiding a potential threat, like the breast tumour Rennie so fears in *Bodily Harm*.

Maternity in particular recurrently figures in Atwood's fiction, though it has an ambiguous status. Women's power to bear children is occasionally a source of puzzlement and wonder. In *Surfacing*, the narrator envisions her pregnancy as part of a healing process that will help her undo the deadening effect of a previous abortion; it is an affirmation and celebration of life. Nevertheless, it is shown too as the root of much oppression: uncontrolled fertility kills women in *Alias Grace*. The need for women to have power over their own bodies is uppermost in Margaret Atwood's writing.

Female villains

The exploitation of women is not men's exclusive province. Not all villains in her fiction are male. From time to time, a female villain appears, indicating thus that women can be cruel too, that they may engage in power politics as well. *Cat's Eye* (1988) is a good example of how even children can terrorize other children; here Cordelia relentlessly torments Elaine, making her feel inadequate. The same topic recurs in *The Robber Bride* (1993), where Zenia systematically takes away from her friends what they most desire: lovers, self-respect, academic success, etc. What makes Zenia such a dangerous villain is precisely her uncanny ability to deploy power like a man, while displaying the endearing attitudes of a woman.

As a matter of fact, villains are shown to be somehow redundant in Atwood's tales. Since they only have the power their victims grant them, women's own passivity and collusion in their own bondage is far more dangerous than anything a villain (male or female) can ever do. All in all, the lesson to be learnt from these novels is that women's solidarity is the only recipe against oppression, while by silence and inaction they contribute to it. The problem is that women sometimes prefer not to see. It's easier.

WAYS OF SEEING

Atwood's women characters are often artists. They have been trained to look at the world and to capture it in images or in words. Joan in *Lady Oracle* and Iris in *The Blind Assassin* are writers; Lesjie in *Life Before Man* and Tony in *The Robber Bride* are academics; Elaine in *Cat's Eye* is a painter. Other characters display artistic talent but have never managed to develop it, like Grace in *Alias Grace*. Occasionally, these women feel they have betrayed the high call and fulfilment of art for the stability of a paying job, like the unnamed narrator of *Surfacing*, who is a children's book illustrator, or Rennie in *Bodily Harm*, who writes cheery travel pieces for women's magazines.

Whether by nature or by training, these women have the ability to see beyond appearances, but for some reason they fail to see themselves clearly. Facing a decisive moment in their lives, they can't see a way out. They think they can't read or interpret people and things around them properly. They just don't have enough information to go by. Should Offred trust the Commander, or Nick, in *The Handmaid's Tale*? Are people telling the truth or elaborate lies? What is the meaning of a gesture, a sign? Is there an ulterior motive? Looking and seeing are not the same thing, and Atwood's characters agonize over the choices they are forced to make, and over the risks each of them entails.

Art and reality

Art sometimes appears as a way to control reality, or at least if offers the illusion of control. In the short story 'Death by Landscape', Lois has long been an art collector. Although most of her friends admire her for what they consider a sound investment, the paintings of landscapes on her apartment walls represent her method to tame a wilderness that she finds frightening. She has never gone north since she was 13. That year, at summer camp, her best friend Lucy vanished during a canoe trip. Her disappearance was never satisfactorily explained, and in the paintings Lois is endlessly looking for the lost Lucy. Art helps her come to terms with a much larger reality.

While writing or painting are acceptable in Atwood's fiction, photos awaken distrust because they are artificial and mechanical artefacts. They are perceived as an illegitimate means of appropriating what is seen. They become phallic symbols and aggressive weapons, especially in men's hands. In *The Edible Woman*, Peter's cameras are kept in his bedroom, close to his hunting rifles:

To one side of the bookcase is a pegboard with hooks that holds Peter's collection of weapons: two rifles, a pistol, and several wicked-looking knives. I've been told all the names, but I can never remember them. I've never seen Peter use any of them, though of course in the city he wouldn't have many opportunities. Apparently he used to go hunting with his oldest friends. Peter's cameras hang there too, their glass eyes covered by leather cases.

(*The Edible Woman*, ch. 7)

Clearly, Marian feels uncomfortable about these 'glass eyes' watching her from under the leather. Photography freezes the object in a certain time and place, and in that sense, it 'kills' as much as a gun would, though in a different way. That is the reason why Marian finally flees and breaks her engagement when Peter tries to take a picture of her. In *Surfacing*, David has rented a video-camera for his project 'Random Samples'. By filming unrelated scenes, places or people, David is objectifying them, appropriating them, and ultimately denying their very existence. This technique of fragmentation and consumption is more evident when he demands that his wife Anna pose naked for the film.

Looking and seeing

David is not the only character that fails to see the big picture. Many are incapable of looking beyond their immediate surroundings. They look, but they can't see. There is in Atwood's work an implied criticism of people's parochialism, but other characters experience the frustration of their desire to see. The best example is the handmaids' head dress in *The Handmaid's Tale*, whose wings impose strict limits on the women's roving eyes. Like other essential freedoms, in Gilead the power to look (and to manipulate others' sight) belongs only to men.

If people can only see part of the picture, then it follows that everything is a matter of perspective. No two people would give the same account of an event they had witnessed. What and how we see affects our experiences and our lives. As a result, there are as many stories as people. Atwood's fiction often provides separate points of view for the same events – this is known as **perspectivism**. In *Life Before Man,* for example, a love triangle unfolds through the voices of the three characters. In *The Robber Bride* too, three voices describe the same person, but the result is so different that it might as well be another person altogether.

> **KEYWORD**
>
> Perspectivism: The belief that there is no absolute truth. Everything is subjective, the result of each individual perspective.

However, this is not necessarily wrong. Human beings are by nature imperfect and limited. Only machines can grasp and handle a complete view of things or events, but they are not human. When people attempt to be completely objective, they often become inhuman, because they are losing sight of the human element and behaving with the coldness of machines. In *The Handmaid's Tale*, the historian Piexoto deplores that Offred's account left out many valuable data and instead focused on trivia. But by looking down on Offred he is refusing to learn the lesson she has tried to convey, and is also denying the pain and suffering of many other women.

If subjectivity can't be helped and objectivity is not even desirable, then how can we get at the truth? Atwood's way of solving this paradox is through plurality. By putting together many partial views of the same event, we will see it from many different sides, and be able to reconstruct a fuller view. That is the closest we can ever get at the truth. This emphasis on plurality is a feature Atwood's work shares with other postmodern authors.

STORYTELLING

Margaret Atwood's fiction is most often written in the first person. 'Fiction,' she says, 'is where individual memory and experience and collective memory and experience come together' (*In Search of Alias Grace* (University of Ottawa Press, 1997), p. 3). Individual memory and experience are the province of Atwood's female narrators, for whom telling stories is an act of survival, the proof that they really exist. The use of the first person by the narrator makes readers feel closer to her experiences. Occasionally, Atwood also introduces a second person, 'you', that involves readers even more. Then 'I' (protagonist, narrator) and 'you' (readers, audience) engage in a conversation, a dialogue:

> You don't tell a story only to yourself. There's always someone else. Even when there is no one. A story is like a letter. *Dear you*, I'll say. Just *you*, without a name … *You* can mean more than one. *You* can mean thousands.
>
> (*The Handmaid's Tale*, ch. 7)

These narrators continue to spin their tales even though sometimes they are not certain whether or not what they remember and what happened are the same. Human memory is an unreliable tool, and at best, it can perform only an imperfect reconstruction of the past, as Offred admits:

> It didn't happen that way either. I'm not sure how it happened; not exactly. All I can hope for is a reconstruction: the way love feels is always only approximate.
>
> (*The Handmaid's Tale*, ch. 40)

Postmodern metafiction

This explicit preoccupation with the ambiguous status of the story one is telling is characteristic of postmodern metafiction, as we saw previously. Since their stories are always about the past, about events that continue to haunt them in the present, Atwood's narrators are eventually unable to distinguish fact from fiction. Actually, it does not matter whether something really happened in a particular way. Everything is just a reconstruction, tales they endlessly rehearse in the hope that someone will listen. Being listened to is important because they aspire to transmit not just their individual memories or experiences, but also those of other people. They feel they have the duty to give testimony about their society and times, especially as they affect women. Their voices are at the same time single and collective.

Therefore, Atwood's fiction turns to be not just about individual issues, but about the larger society too. Further indication of this is how she weaves many other tales into hers. There are constant allusions in her work to other cultural artefacts, ranging from television programmes to popular songs, advertisements, paintings, and of course literature. This wealth of references to other texts is known as **intertextuality**.

Only those readers who are familiar with the intertext (the song, advertisement, poem, etc.), to which the new text alludes can enjoy that added layer of meaning. For example, in *Alias Grace* each chapter is introduced by a quilt pattern (a 'visual' text) and one or more quotes (a 'linguistic' text) that we are meant to interpret and relate to the contents of the chapter. In this novel, many of the intertexts can be traced to nineteenth-century works. This frequently happens in Atwood.

Other popular Atwoodian intertexts are children's literature, like Lewis Carroll's *Alice in Wonderland* and fairytales. Occasionally, the relevance of the intertext grows to such an extent that the author is in fact offering a new rendering of it: a **rewriting**. Atwood has published several rewritings, especially of the fairytale of **Bluebeard**, which she made over in her story 'Bluebeard's Egg' and in her novel *The Robber Bride*. At other times she has rewritten **canonical works**, like Shakespeare's plays.

KEYWORD

Intertextuality: A characteristic of much postmodern literature. It consists of the insertion of references and allusions to previous texts in another.

Rewriting: A technique consisting in telling an old story from a new, fresh perspective. Postmodern authors use it in order to question the ideas and messages implied in the old texts. It is also considered a feminist device, especially since Adrienne Rich's famous essay 'When We Dead Awaken' (1976).

Bluebeard: A traditional fairytale about a man who married women and then murdered them. There are several versions of the tale bearing different titles, like Perrault's 'Bluebeard' and the Brothers Grimm's 'Fitcher's Egg' and 'The Robber Bridegroom'.

Canonical works: Works of art that are considered outstanding and therefore have entered the list of best works in the history of humanity, or 'canon'.

In the short story 'Gertrude Talks Back', Hamlet's mother gets to tell her side of the story, why she married Claudius and what she really thinks about her son, but only those who are familiar with Shakespeare's *Hamlet* can understand the full impact of the revelations made by Atwood's Gertrude.

Atwood also likes to play with the conventions of different literary genres. For example, she employs the structure of detective stories in many of her novels, but she does not respect their rules. She may tell us from the beginning who the murderer is, but not why. She shifts from one genre to another: a science fiction tale may be inserted inside a larger narrative frame (*The Blind Assassin*). Finally, she also likes to mingle different kinds of materials. Side by side with more traditional narrative sections, we may encounter excerpts from newspapers, diaries or letters.

✱ ✱ ✱ *SUMMARY* ✱ ✱ ✱

Some major themes in Atwood's fiction are:

● the use of Gothic elements, particularly in the plot and setting of the novels

● the emphasis on women's painful experiences

● that human perception is by nature limited and imperfect and machines can't be trusted

● that memory is at the same time individual and collective.

5 Major Works

EARLY NOVELS

Margaret Atwood's early novels came soon after her success as a poet; they introduced some of her lifelong preoccupations as a writer. In *The Edible Woman*, she explores issues of power and the construction of femininity; in *Surfacing*, she first uses the occurrence of a mysterious death to build suspense and to engage readers in a detective quest; in *Lady Oracle* she plays with literary genres and conventions.

The Edible Woman (1969)

Atwood's first novel deals with the problems of a young woman who feels strong societal pressures to conform. It is a ***Bildungsroman***, focusing on the development of Marian MacAlpin from a fairly conventional girl into a self-reliant woman. Marian works for a consumer surveys company, and so she is used

> **KEYWORD**
>
> *Bildungsroman*: A novel focusing on a character's personal growth, psychological or physical, or both.

to quizzing people on their likes and dislikes, but she herself has not seriously considered where her life is going. Like most people around her, she has assumed she is going to work only until she gets married to a proper young man and has nice tidy children. However, as that moment approaches and her relationship with Peter turns more serious, she starts having second thoughts.

Female role models

There are no positive female role models around Marian. Her best friend Clara married very young and gave up college. She is expecting her third child and lives in a messy house surrounded by messy little children. To Marian, she resembles a queen ant, and she is faintly repelled by Clara's body, that 'seemed somehow beyond her, going its own way without reference to any directions of hers' (ch. 4). On the contrary, Marian's roommate Ainsley is too much in control. She has decided that she wants to have a baby on her own, and she puts on an elaborate masquerade in order to entrap an appropriate biological father. She is compared to 'a general plotting a major campaign' (ch. 10). Marian's friends at work are no better. Known collectively as 'the office virgins', these women's sole objective is to get married. Finally, Marian's landlady polices the behaviour of her tenants, deciding what is proper and decent for young single women to do.

So far, Marian has accepted other people's expectations and shaped herself accordingly. This is most true in the case of her boyfriend, Peter, who often congratulates her on her 'common sense', by which he really means that she is submissive and undemanding. Marian is a new *Alice in Wonderland*. Like Alice, she is bewildered by people's beliefs and attitudes, which often seem bizarre to her. But like Alice too, she accepts the rules of the land without question, becoming bigger or smaller as others see fit. In a world where people are either hunters or prey, she is the latter.

The novel is divided into three sections. The first one, written in the first person, ends with Marian's engagement to Peter. In the next, Atwood shifts to the third person, hinting that Marian is alienated from her true self, and not

KEYWORD

Alice's Adventures in Wonderland: A classic children's novel written by the Victorian mathematician Lewis Carroll in 1865, describing the adventures of seven-year-old Alice as she falls down a rabbit hole and into a fantasy world full of bizarre characters, where what she eats or drinks makes her change size to adapt to her surroundings.

Anorexia nervosa: An eating disorder, common among adolescents, in which the sufferer gives up eating.

in control of her own story/body. Throughout that section, she finds herself unable to eat certain foods. It starts with red meat, but as her wedding day approaches, she can eat virtually nothing. Marian is experiencing an eating disorder known as **anorexia nervosa**. The disease is a symptom of her psychological dilemma. She refuses to consume because she sides with the consumed. She grows more and more passive with each passing day, while everyone else seems satisfied.

The only person near her who is outside the system, living by his own set of rules, is Duncan. He is a graduate student Marian met by chance. She is mystified by his bizarre behaviour and his total disregard of all social conventions. She also feels that Duncan can see her true self. Marian starts a relationship with him as an antidote to Peter, but Duncan does not want to be anyone's knight in shining armour. At the end of section two, Marian has finally realized that she must take control of her own life. She goes home and bakes a woman-shaped cake, then invites her fiancé Peter for coffee and cake and accuses him of wanting to destroy her:

> 'You've been trying to destroy me, haven't you?', she said. 'You've been trying to assimilate me. But I've made you a substitute, something you'll like much better. This is what you wanted all along, isn't it?'
>
> (*The Edible Woman*, ch. 30)

By breaking off her engagement in this unconventional way, Marian feels liberated and healed. The final section shifts again to the first person because Marian has regained control of her life. The last scene shows her cleaning out the apartment, a symbol of her putting her life in order.

Surfacing (1972)

With her second novel, Margaret Atwood won wide acclaim. *Surfacing* continues to be listed among her best work.

A journey of discovery

The novel is consistently told in the first person by an unnamed female narrator, sometimes termed 'the surfacer' in critical essays. It is structured as a **quest narrative**, with the narrator travelling back from the city into the Quebec bush in search of her missing father.

> **KEYWORD**
>
> Quest narrative: A narrative form structured around a voyage of discovery. The voyage may be literal or psychological, and the discovery may be of something internal or external to the quester. Generally the quest heals the quester and helps him/her go back home renewed.

This journey also takes her back into a former, happier life and self, when she used to live there with her family.

The surfacer returns to this scenery riddled with painful memories and experiences. She left home in order to take up a relationship with her art teacher, a married man who forced her to have an abortion. The resulting trauma left her numbed, unable to return home and incapable of feeling love again. Although she took up with another man, her current lover Joe, she feels unable to reach out to him. She keeps her distance from acquaintances like David and Anna, the married couple who drive them to her father's cabin to help her search for clues to his whereabouts. She has lost touch with her art, too, and makes a living by providing cute illustrations for children's books.

Looking and seeing are two activities at the heart of this novel. The surfacer looks for clues all around her. Apparently, these can help her discover what happened to her father, but more and more it becomes clear that this is in fact a search for self-discovery. Like the narrator, the landscape of lakes and cabins has suffered the ravages of time and the aggressions of other people. The aggressors are identified as 'Americans', but Atwood is not simply staking a nationalist claim. Some of the more destructive tourists turn out to be Canadian. 'American' is a label for all those people, whatever their nationality, who behave without the proper regard to the environment and to other people's needs. It may also be a label for David, whose camera is an unwelcome intruder, and who uses those around him for his own ends. Not surprisingly, the narrator ends up destroying the film David has been shooting.

Most of the clues around the surfacer are graphic. She finds drawings and scrapbooks, photo albums and Native inscriptions, some left behind by her father, others by her younger self. She agonizes over their meaning and purpose, she follows each sign only to find a closed end, and little by little readers can perceive that she is becoming lost in the quest. Finally, when strangers find her father's drowned body, she refuses to accept his death, and she hides in the woods so that she does not have to go back to the city with the others.

Retreat into Nature

The final stage of her quest quite literally takes her into the wood, as she retreats into a natural lifestyle and cleanses herself from her civilized, city self. She makes a fire and burns most of the items of her past life, the children's book she was working on, the wedding ring her first lover had given her, the photo albums, etc. Alone in the wilderness, she gives up living under shelter, sleeps in the open, goes around naked, eats only the vegetables and berries she can find. Her final retreat into madness deprives her of language.

> The animals have no need for speech, why talk when you are
> a word
> I lean against a tree, I am a tree leaning

I break out again into the bright sun and crumple, head against
  the ground
I am not an animal or a tree, I am the thing in which the trees
and animals move and grow, I am a place.

(Surfacing, ch. 24)

During this period she has visions of her dead parents. First she can see
her mother feeding the birds in front of the cabin, as she used to do in
the past, and later on she sees her father looking in at the garden. These
two visions represent the reconnection with the past that the surfacer
has been looking for all along. They bring about a healing and a sense
of closure, and so the narrator feels ready to go back to the city and
start over again. Her psychological rebirth is conveyed through her
commitment to her lover and through her pregnancy. Both symbolize
a reclamation of the self, as well as a reaffirmation of life over death.
The quest is now complete, and the quester can return to society
equipped with new power and knowledge.

Lady Oracle (1976)

Lady Oracle is among Atwood's most popular novels, probably because
of its powerful comedy. It is truly an enjoyable read, and as such the
novel gives the impression of being simple. However, a second reading
reveals that Atwood is working with very complex materials and
combining different generic conventions.

The novel starts with the stunning revelation 'I planned my death
carefully' (ch. 1), which establishes the unusual fact that the narrator,
Joan Foster, has faked her death in Lake Ontario in order to escape a
life that she couldn't control. Having safely reached a little town in
Italy, she spends some time thinking things over but eventually she
hears that her friends have been accused of murdering her, and so she
decides to go back to clear things up.

A comic heroine

In the central sections of the novel, Joan's confessional voice leads the
readers through the maze of her past life and her multiple

personalities. Her mother named her after the actress Joan Crawford, an early indication of the high expectations she had for her daughter, but the child Joan was found wanting in grace and beauty. She was an ugly duckling that never managed to meet her mother's desires. As she grew into adolescence, Joan started overeating as a way to annoy and defy her. This former self the mature Joan identifies as 'the Fat Lady'.

Joan became a new person with the assistance of her Aunt Lou, an alternative maternal figure. At her death, Aunt Louisa left her a large sum of money on condition she lost weight. As soon as she could, Joan used the money to move out of her home and far from her mother. She travels to Britain, and in London she meets Paul, the Polish Count, who tutors her in sex and writing. Paul makes a living by writing nurse novels, and so when Aunt Lou's money runs out, Joan decides to try her hand at historical romances. This is the beginning of another alter-ego, the historical romance writer Louisa K. Delacourt (her aunt's real name).

Nevertheless, Joan is not proud of her writing, and when she falls in love with and marries Arthur Foster, she hides this fact from him. Yet another personality results from an experiment with automatic writing, and the manuscript is published as a poetry collection, *Lady Oracle*. She is welcomed by the media as a new, intriguing poetess. In this Lady Oracle persona, she begins an affair with another artist, the Royal Porcupine. She is followed by a journalist, Fraser Buchanan, who discovers both the affair and her secret pen name. It is to avoid his blackmail that Joan fakes her death with the help of a friend.

Gothic intertextuality
Interspersed with these memories are fragments of the manuscripts Joan is working on, pieces out of her historical romances. These novels follow the simplest conventions of the Gothic. There is a dark, imposing mansion, a young beautiful orphan who is under threat, a sexually aggressive other woman, and an attractive lord of the house who appears to be the villain but ends up being a hero. Such fragments appear more often as Joan's confession unfolds, and the events of her

real life intrude in the text in progress, shaping both the incidents and the characters. Joan is manifesting her paranoia in her writing, and the other way round, the Gothic is feeding her paranoia. Like the character of Charlotte in the novel she's writing, Joan has entered a labyrinth and can't find her way out.

Joan's problems stem from her inner conflict between career and domesticity. These two extremes are represented by her childhood influences: her mother and Aunt Lou. The former educated her for love and marriage, though she herself was not happy. She experienced a deep dissatisfaction and a rage at the uselessness of her own life, that Joan only uncovered after her death. Looking at the family album, she finds that her mother has cut off the heads of her husband and an earlier boyfriend in all the photos:

> There was only my mother, young and pretty, laughing gaily at the camera, clutching the arms of her headless men. I sat for an hour with the album open on the table before me, stunned by this evidence of her terrible anger. I could almost see her doing it, her long fingers working with precise fury, excising the past, which had turned into the present and betrayed her, stranding her in this house, this plastic-shrouded tomb from which there was no exit.
>
> (*Lady Oracle*, ch. 17)

The opposite impulse, towards career and financial independence, is embodied by Aunt Lou, who holds a good job and lives according to her own terms. After her husband left her, Aunt Lou built a new life for herself, including a boyfriend who is also married. She is a constant source of inspiration for Joan, edging her to move on and do things for herself, but Joan, unlike her aunt, is incapable of reconciling her love life and a fulfilling career, and hides her manuscripts in her underwear drawer.

The conflict between love and career is present in a very relevant intertext, the 1946 film *The Red Shoes*, starring Moira Shearer as an accomplished dancer whose husband does not allow her to continue dancing. Forced to choose between one or the other, she commits suicide. In *Lady Oracle*, Atwood has produced a comic rewriting of the film. The issues remain the same, but she has avoided the drama and pathos of the film. Instead of a real suicide, a fake one. Instead of a talented dancer, a romance writer. Her character makes a mess of all her decisions, but at least she keeps trying.

BODY POLITICS

After the popular success of Lady Oracle, Atwood's fiction shifted to new territories. In particular, her interest in body politics continued to grow. In the next few novels, she addressed issues connected mainly to the female body and to feminist politics. In *Life Before Man* and *The Handmaid's Tale*, her focus is on motherhood and mother–child relationships, while in *Bodily Harm* the female body suffers internal and external threats. Also, she experimented more and more with the creation of point of view and the narrative frames in her novels.

Life Before Man (1979)

Although *Life Before Man* also features a violent death, Atwood did not use it here in order to create a mystery or to build tension, which might explain why this was her least successful novel. The suicide of Chris, Elizabeth Schoenhof's discarded lover, is the starting point for a period of crisis in the life of Elizabeth, her husband Nate, and his new partner Lesje. Elizabeth and Nate have been growing apart for some time but they decided to continue to live in the same house, ostensibly for the sake of their two daughters. Chris's growing demands on Elizabeth's time, and his unwelcome insistence that she leave her husband and daughters and move in with him, led her to break up the relationship. After his death, Elizabeth enters a long period of depression. Nate's hopes that they can still go back together are disappointed by Elizabeth's listlessness, and he finds himself free to try for a new relationship. The novel covers the subtle readjustments deriving from the setting up of the resulting two households.

The personal growth of Nate, Elizabeth and Lesje takes place roughly over a period of two years, from October 1976 to August 1978. The characters tell their own side of the story in chapters resembling diary entries because they are clearly identified with their name and date, though they are written in the third person. Atwood's objective is to balance the different perspectives so that readers can see the three sides, while bringing us as close as possible to the minds of the characters.

Childhood traumas
The main characters have a lot in common. All three experienced miserable childhoods, and they need to overcome deep traumas, the effects of which show up whenever they encounter difficulties. Until now, they have found ways to retreat from the pain, but none to solve the problem. Each of them must eventually face and destroy a demon that has haunted them for years.

Elizabeth's family broke up when her father left them and her mother started drinking. She and her younger sister Caroline were then taken in and later formally adopted by their Auntie Muriel, their mother's sister. Although the children were given everything money and respectability could buy, they were deeply unhappy by the desertion of their mother and the lack of love in their new home. Caroline had to be committed to an institution, where she accidentally died. Elizabeth has survived by growing a thick skin over her feelings of inadequacy and guilt because she failed to keep her family together and to protect her younger sister. She has also tried to meet the exacting demands of Auntie Muriel, holding a steady job and maintaining the appearance of a respectable family even though she has long stopped loving her husband. When she had trouble coping, she took up with men she found attractive because they represented an alternative lifestyle: low class, improper, unrespectable. But these minor escapes are shattered by Chris's suicide. When Nate moves out, Elizabeth finally has to confront Auntie Muriel, and this is a first step towards a real independence of mind. Her aunt's last illness and death soon after also help her rethink her childhood and her relationship with both her biological and her adoptive mother in more positive terms.

Nate's father died in World War II when Nate was a baby, and he grew up under the shadow of a hero. Like Elizabeth, he has always felt inadequate. He couldn't live up to the expectations of his mother, a woman who has always been committed to larger causes, ranging from war veterans to hunger in faraway countries. He became a lawyer due to his mother's notions, but his growing cynicism has made him give up the law and become a toy-maker, carving wooden horses in the basement of the house he continues to share with his estranged wife. He has been inhabiting a sort of no man's land, retreating from their shared bedroom into the guest bedroom, and from the larger world into the basement. Finally, his new relationship with Lesje forces him to take some radical decisions and to go out into the world once more. He also starts reconsidering his social role when he realizes that his mother's commitments are not caused by her moral superiority but by her need to fill the huge void the death of her husband left her with.

Lesje is the only daughter of unlikely parents: a Jewish father and a Ukrainian mother. Their history of racial hatred in Europe followed the two families to Canada, and was embodied by the enmity of Lesje's two grandmothers, who fought endlessly over the girl. She too grew up in a kind of blank, because in order to avoid confrontations her parents adopted the traditions of the Anglo culture neither of them belonged to by birth. As a result, Lesje is deprived of the language and heritage of both family groups, feeling equally lost in both. She early found escape from these conflicts in her visits to the Royal Ontario Museum, a place of science and knowledge. She thus developed an interest in dinosaurs and became a paleontologist. When under pressure, Lesje retreated into a dream land populated by dinosaurs. Nevertheless, her relationship with a man who comes with two daughters and a former wife makes escape impossible. Although at first she experiences a growing antagonism for Elizabeth, she finally realizes that by fighting over Nate, the two women would repeat the actions of her two grandmothers. She too must grow up and move beyond those demons.

There are many intertextual references in the novel. Since *Life Before Man* deals with the traumas of childhood, there are recurrent allusions to two popular children's books, *Alice in Wonderland* (especially for Lesje, whose name is the Ukrainian equivalent of 'Alice' and would like to live in the time of the dinosaurs) and *The Wizard of Oz* (for Elizabeth, who feels an orphan and would like to kill the evil witch, as well as for Nate, who sees himself as ineffectual as the Scarecrow).

Bodily Harm (1981)

Bodily Harm has much in common with the short story 'A Travel Piece', published in Atwood's 1977 collection, *Dancing Girls*. Both feature woman journalists who specialize in 'light' pieces for fashion magazines. They write what people want to read, and they prefer not to look hard at anything that is disagreeable, unfashionable or otherwise painful. Like other Atwood characters they are, or attempt to be, spectators who can pass through life without suffering, hidden away behind a camera or a notebook. Writing provides them with a detachment they need.

KEY FACT

The Wizard of Oz: Another classic children's tale, by American writer L. Frank Baum in 1900. The 1939 film version, a musical starring Judy Garland, made it very popular. Dorothy, an orphan Kansas girl, travels to the City of Emeralds, ruled by the famous Wizard of Oz, whose magic can perform miracles for her and her companions, the Scarecrow (who wants brains), the Tin Woodman (who needs a heart), and the Lion (who lacks courage). But the Wizard is not a magician, only an illusionist. Atwood has discussed this story in *Negotiating with the Dead* (2002).

Violence against women

In both cases, events force these women to come out of hiding, and to reconsider their lives. Rennie Wilford, the protagonist of the novel, travels to the Caribbean island of St. Antoine in search of a retreat, a paradise of sun and sand. Her life is a mess. She has recently undergone surgery for breast cancer, and feels her body violated. The invasion of her home by a man who is stalking her is one trespass too many. Rennie is surrounded by violence, especially violence directed towards women. *Bodily Harm* resembles *The Edible Woman*, because here Atwood takes another turn at the problem of images of women in popular culture. A case in point is an exhibition of pornographic objects seized by the police that she visited. Her reaction was to pretend such violence just doesn't exist.

> Rennie decided that there were some things it was better not to know any more about than you had to. Surfaces, in many cases, were preferable to depths. She did a piece on the return of the angora sweater, and another one on the handknit-look industry. That was soothing. There was much to be said for trivia.
>
> (*Bodily Harm*, ch. 5)

By preferring not to look, Rennie has given up control over her life little by little. First she let her lover Jake take decisions for her: what she should wear, what her home should look like, etc. A designer by trade, Jake shaped her after his own fantasies, which were at times fairly violent. Later, when she was diagnosed with cancer, she transferred those powers to her doctor, Daniel, who had performed the miracle of rescuing her from near death.

She has nightmares that she is cut open, and that there are maggots eating her up from the inside. Rennie's sex life is seriously affected. At the literal level, Atwood explores the loss of self-confidence that many survivors of breast cancer suffer. However, her disease is also used as a metaphor for her crippling, alienating philosophy. She is more and more cut off from herself and from other women. Another recurrent dream is of her grandmother, who in later life used to go around looking for her hands, thinking she had misplaced them. Similarly, Rennie has lost the power to touch other people. She is faintly disgusted by other women's hands. She finds them too pathetic, or like her own, too ineffectual. Men's hands, however, are active and powerful: they shape things, they hold guns, they cut people's bodies.

Rennie's hope that she can heal in the Caribbean is not justified. The island is in turmoil. Two parties are fighting over control of the government; American and Canadian 'tourists' trade in guns and drugs; the police beat up people in the streets. Rennie is innocently taken in by other people's plots, and she ends up in prison. Although this could be seen as the worst possible fate, it proves to be Rennie's salvation, a true re-birth as her name 'Re-nata' indicates. Sharing a cell with Lora, a woman she is acquainted with but feels little sympathy for, it dawns on her that they have something in common after all. Rennie learns the value of female solidarity, and she finally 'grows' hands again and reaches out to another woman.

The personal is political

Remarkably, solidarity in the novel results from telling stories. The novel is divided into several sections which usually start with a first-person statement introducing a narrative. For example, Section 1 opens with: ' "This is how I got here," says Rennie.' As we read on, we can finally understand that these fragments are the stories about themselves that the two women share as a way to pass the time in their cell. These tales make evident that they both have more in common than they had ever expected, mostly in that they suffered and continue to suffer abuse and violence at the hands of men.

Bodily Harm focuses on contents and plots that are more openly political than in earlier fiction by Atwood. It looks at the role and actions of Canadians in relation to other parts of the world, as well as examining the situation of women from a more global perspective. The shift from the national to the international continues in Atwood's following work.

The Handmaid's Tale (1985)

In this novel, Atwood experimented with a new genre, **dystopia**. The story is set in the United States in an unspecified future. A religious faction has taken over the government and suppressed most civil liberties, building a fundamentalist social order where women have no rights. In a world where pollution and toxic waste have affected the birth rate, women who can still bear healthy children have become a valuable commodity. As such, the 'Handmaids' are placed in the households of powerful childless men ('Commanders'). Each month on a fertile night, the Handmaid must have sex with her Commander in the presence of his Wife ('the Ceremony'). If she can perform the miracle of conceiving and carrying to term his child, the Handmaid's

KEYWORD

Dystopia: A genre used to examine social issues. Dystopian works describe an imaginary world full of negative features. Usually, the citizens of such worlds live under a tyrannical rule (e.g. George Orwell's *1984*) or in an impersonal, mechanized society (e.g. Aldous Huxley's *Brave New World*) where human life and needs have little worth.

future is safe. If she can't, she is classified as an 'Unwoman' (a worthless female) and sent to the Colonies, where she dies a premature death due to exposure to radiation.

Women and religion

Atwood's inspiration for the writing of this claustrophobic tale comes from several sources. Her imaginary society, Gilead, is a Christian fundamentalism, and so it is partly based on the Puritan period in the United States. She dedicated the novel to Professor Perry Miller, who taught her American Literature at Harvard, and to her ancestor Mary Webster, who survived the witch hunt in late seventeenth-century New England. Closer to her own times, she drew some of her inspiration from the political changes in Iran in 1979, when that country became an Islamic Republic. Similarly, the fact that she partly wrote the novel during a visit to Berlin surely had an impact on some of its features, especially in her description of 'the Wall'.

The figure and role of the Handmaid derives from the Bible. Atwood has inserted a quote from Genesis that describes how Rachel despaired from giving her husband Jacob children, and so she asked him to take her maid Bilhah in her place. Bilhah's children would be Rachel's, just like the Handmaid in the novel is seen as a mere chattel, and her role subordinate to that of the Commander and his Wife. The Bible is often quoted in the novel, a major instrument for teaching the Handmaids to submit to men. The Gilead regime has manipulated its fundamental text to make it more suitable to its ends. For instance, the possessive pronouns in one of the slogans have been altered:

> *From each*, says the slogan, *according to her ability; to each according to his needs.* We recited that, three times, after dessert. It was from the Bible, or so they said. St. Paul again, in Acts.
>
> (*The Handmaid's Tale*, ch. 20)

As it reads now, women are the only ones to give, men always the ones who receive. This subtle rewriting is made possible by the prohibition on women to read and write, so they can never check the actual words.

Language and power
Language is under scrutiny in *The Handmaid's Tale*, as is often the case in dystopic novels. Atwood explores the potential of language both for subversion and rebellion, and for tyranny. The Gilead regime manipulates and censors all means of communication, subjecting its citizens to constant surveillance, and limiting people's (particularly women's) access to information. Talking has become dangerous, and real communication is hindered by the use of formulas, often religious in tone or precedence. For example, 'Blessed be the fruit' is the accepted greeting among Handmaids, and 'May the Lord open' the proper reply. In such a context, the mere possession of a book or even a pen is enough to send a woman to the Colonies.

This concern is conveyed through the voice of the narrator, a Handmaid posted in the household of a Commander named Fred. She receives the name Offred ('of-fred') after her Commander, while her real name is never disclosed. She also bears a tattooed number on an ankle. Both are symbols of her oppression in a patriarchal system. For this narrator, telling her story is a means of survival, a way to remain sane in a world that has suddenly gone crazy. She has lost everything she cared for: home, family, job, friends. Moreover, she is on her third and final posting. If she cannot provide the system with a child, she will die. By telling her story she strives to make sense of the past and of her present life, and she imagines a companion she can tell her worries to. Also, telling a story is a means of detaching oneself from experiences that are too real and too painful to the teller. That is why the narrative is interspersed with comments on the tale itself and the nature of storytelling. This kind of self-reflective narrative is known as metafiction.

History versus stories
Offred's voice is framed by a final section entitled 'Historical Notes'. This is a piece of academic writing, quite different in tone from her testimony. It is a lecture on Gilead during a symposium held in 2195.

Professor Piexoto explains that her story was found hidden away in Maine, recorded in tapes that he and a colleague have transcribed and edited. This is Atwood's way of providing other perspectives on the same experience, as she consistently does in her fiction. It is also a method she uses to contrast the apparent objectivity of the academic lecture and the apparent subjectivity of the first-hand account. Piexoto's point is that we should not censure, but understand ('Historical Notes on *The Handmaid's Tale*'). However, this is ironical, because the whole point of Offred's story is that commitment is necessary, and that watching someone's pain and remaining inactive is wrong. As usual in Atwood's work, objectivity is a fake, hiding a bias that is often patriarchal (note Piexoto's sexist jokes, for instance).

History as an allegedly objective narrative of events is counteracted by a plurality of stories. Offred's account of her life resonates with the sufferings of other women characters too. It has the power of the shared experience. She represents the average white woman leading the average middle-class life, who suddenly wakes up to a nightmarish situation. She is surrounded by more radical characters (her friend Moira and her mother) as well as by more traditional ones (Serena Joy and Janine).

Portraits of women
Moira is one of Atwood's most engaging creations, a woman whose wit, courage and determination make her a source of inspiration for those who won't submit to this authoritarian system. Offred's unnamed mother is a portrait of the committed feminist who fought for gender equality in the 1960s and 1970s, and who watches younger women like her own daughter enjoy those advantages without caring to preserve them. By means of these two models of resistance against patriarchy, the novel emphasizes that equality must continue to be fought for; the task is never quite finished.

Very far from them in attitudes and values are the two other major female characters. Serena Joy is the former name of the Commander's

Wife. She embodies the fate of those women who believe in the traditional roles of mother and wife. She fought for this cause just as Offred's mother had fought for the opposite one, but she has been pushed aside by the system and forced to lead an aimless life. She has become an embittered woman, who spends her days knitting endless scarves and doing the gardening. Janine is an example of what total submission to a patriarchal system can do to women. Like Offred, she just wants to survive, but she will go to any lengths necessary to ensure survival. Her fate is worse than death. It's the total loss of identity.

The Handmaid's Tale masterfully highlights many of the themes and topics that Atwood had contemplated in her earlier works, in particular the victimization of women and the treacherous quality of the female body. Red is a recurrent colour in this novel, associated to the Handmaids' dress, flowers, menstruation and physical violence.

TORONTO STORIES

After the success of *The Handmaid's Tale*, Atwood wrote two novels where she examined the issue of women's friendship. The setting in both cases is Toronto during the writer's own lifetime. *Cat's Eye* is strongly autobiographical in its portrait of childhood, while *The Robber Bride* tackles the changes in women's lives from the 1960s to the 1990s.

Cat's Eye (1988)

Cat´s Eye is a novel of childhood told from the perspective of middle age. Elaine Risley, a modestly successful painter currently living in Vancouver, returns to the city where she grew up, Toronto, for her first retrospective exhibition. As she prepares for the opening, the city around her brings her back to her former life and to the people in it.

Children's cruelty

Above all, she revisits the psychological torture she suffered at the hands of her three best friends, Cordelia, Grace and Carol. Cordelia was the instigator of cruel games and the other two followed her lead. They judged Elaine deficient in qualities and values that changed from day to day. Whether she passed or failed her exams, walked too fast or too slowly, wore trousers or skirts, Elaine never seemed to meet the demands of her friends. Day after day she kept trying, and the tension of being under the constant inspection of the other girls led her to bite her nails and peel the skin off her feet. At times she even fainted. This secret torture went on day after day, month after month. One day, Cordelia threw Elaine's hat into a ravine where the girls were forbidden to go. In retrieving it, she fell into a creek at the bottom of the ravine, and she was close to frostbite. After this ordeal, she stopped acknowledging Cordelia's power to make her suffer, and cut off all her links with the other girls.

Elaine's mind buried the memories of this pain for a long time, and they did not return until many years later, when in going over some old items kept in the basement she found a beautiful marble, of the kind known as 'cat's eye', which she used to keep as a protecting charm.

However, Elaine can also remember other Cordelias. The girl at high school had changed, and she was now the one found wanting. She failed at school, she seemed disturbed, easily manipulated. She was transferred to another school, where she did not fare any better. She becomes a pathetic shadow of herself. She reappears in Elaine's life from time to time, and after a suicide attempt she is interned in a clinic and kept on tranquillizers.

The novel hints, but never really discloses, that Cordelia's mental instability was triggered by the impossibility of meeting her father's exacting demands. Her cruel games about being disappointed in Elaine echo the ones she herself was a part of at home. This interpretation is also supported by the association of her name with that of King Lear's youngest daughter in Shakespeare's play, the one who loves her father the most, and at the same time the one who can't express her love in the way he expects to hear.

Elaine finally lost track of her, but she remained a powerful presence in her unconscious, a figure that is always close to her field of vision but never quite in it. She thinks she can spot Cordelia in other shapes, other bodies that for a minute resemble the lost friend. Cordelia is Elaine's double, a symbol of her hidden or suppressed side, the capability for good and evil that all human beings carry inside them.

> This is the only picture I ever did of Cordelia, Cordelia by herself. *Half a Face*, it's called: an odd title, because Cordelia's entire face is visible. But behind her, hanging on the wall, like emblems in the Renaissance, or those heads of animals, moose or bear, you used to find in northern bars, is another face, covered with a white cloth. The effect is of a theatrical mask. Perhaps.
>
> (*Cat's Eye*, ch. 41)

The symbolism of art

Elaine's paintings are clues to her mental landscape. In 'Three Muses', for example, she recreates the figures of people who were kind to her in her childhood: a teacher, a neighbour and one of her father's colleagues. 'Three Witches' alludes to her three friends' mothers by representing the three sofas in their homes, each aiming at a lifestyle, an idea of domesticity that has to do with their class origins. Most of all, the series of paintings on Mrs. Smeath is the silent way Elaine manifests her submerged hatred for Grace's mother. A devout Christian, Mrs. Smeath insisted that nine-year-old Elaine came to church every Sunday with them and received the Christian instruction that her parents were not giving her. But after several months of trying hard to become 'a good girl', Elaine finally realized that Mrs. Smeath had known all along about the way the other girls were treating her and had colluded in the torment. At that point the child realized that good Christians could be cruel and evil too.

Towards the end of the novel, Elaine Risley looks around her at the pictures hanging in the still empty gallery, and sees her own past existence in them. The few days needed to prepare the exhibition have given her the time to take stock, and to move on into the future. All in all, the protagonist of *Cat's Eye* feels that she can let go of revenge, and has achieved a maturity and stability that allows her to start the remaining part of her life with serenity and good will.

The Robber Bride (1993)

The three women friends – Tony, Charis and Roz – in *The Robber Bride* share the spotlight with the city of Toronto. The changing appearance of the urban landscape, as well as familiar landmarks like Lake Ontario, Casa Loma or the CN Tower, are not only the background to the story, but they are also significant part of it.

The women grew up in post-World War II Canada, a period of prosperity in which women had to return to the home and fulfil the roles of wives and mothers in a still parochial, close-minded environment. In the downtown campus of the University of Toronto during the 1960s and 1970s, Tony, Roz and Charis met each other and their foe Zenia. They also became members of the counterculture and renovation of customs that characterized university life at the time. Later on, as adult, professional women, they walked the streets of the postmodern, trendy Toronto of the 1980s. The changing city mirrors the women's evolution.

Haunted by the past

Yet, like many other Atwoodian characters, the three friends have suffered a childhood trauma that stalks them and erodes their self-confidence. Each of them has an essential weakness that makes them vulnerable to Zenia's tricks. Tony suffered the desertion of her parents. First, her mother left the home without saying goodbye; later, her father committed suicide. Thus, she feels unworthy of other people's love and she expects to be deserted. The fact that her husband West may leave her for Zenia seems to her entirely logical. Charis (whose real name is Karen) grew up under the care of a cold-hearted aunt and a sexually abusive uncle. A small inheritance from loving grandmother allowed her to break free and reinvent herself, but she never recovered from the trauma of being molested, and she is the most gullible of the three friends, always ready to empathize with the weak and suffering. Roz's early life was full of hardship, and so her father's dubiously acquired wealth came too late to provide her with the self-confidence of an upper-class origin. She is well aware that her husband married her for her money, and though she has become a successful business woman she feels wanting.

Each of them has suffered the deception of a woman who briefly posed as their friend in order to steal from them what they most cherished, their lover, and then discard him and move on. She is the 'robber bride' of the title, since she behaves like the famous Bluebeard figure of the fairy tale '*The Robber Bridegroom*'.

> **KEY FACT**
>
> 'The Robber Bridegroom': A fairytale by the Brothers Grimm about a miller's daughter engaged to a mysterious rich man that turns out to be a thief. Warned by an old woman, she contrives to catch the thief and his band and deliver them to justice.

'*The Robber Bridegroom*,' reads Tony, long ago, a twin at each elbow. The beautiful maiden, the search for a husband, the arrival of the rich and handsome stranger who lures innocent girls to a stronghold in the woods and then chops them up and eats them, 'One day a suitor appeared. He was...'
'She! She!' clamour the twins.
'All right, Tony, let's see you get out of this one,' says Roz, standing in the doorway.
'We could change it to *The Robber Bride*,' says Tony. 'Would that be adequate?'
The twins give it some thought, and say it will do. (...)
The Robber Bride, thinks Roz. Well, why not? Let the grooms take it in the neck for once. The Robber Bride, lurking in her mansion in the dark forest, preying upon the innocent, enticing youths to their doom in her evil cauldron. Like Zenia.

(*The Robber Bride*, ch. 39)

Very little is really known about Zenia besides her name. To each of the women she tells a different story. She creates a different Zenia that they may pity and trust. Nothing reliable is known about her life or background. She is surrounded by mystery, and that makes her even more powerful. Zenia behaves like the women's dark twin. She personifies for each of them what they most lack, fear and admire, a combination that succeeds every time.

Zenia is also a believable creation precisely because she has no voice in the novel. *The Robber Bride* is structured on alternating chapters told from the perspective of each of the three friends, a structure that resembles *Life Before Man*. Zenia appears only in their separate memories, and briefly in some conversations. Strikingly, what each of them remembers is altogether different from the others. This proves that Zenia is ultimately a figment of their imagination, and that 'the real Zenia' must have been someone perhaps altogether different, that they never got to know.

Nevertheless, these three women are a comfort to each other. Surviving Zenia is something they can do because they are together. As usual in Atwood's fiction, solidarity among women helps win the day.

INTO THE HISTORICAL

In her latest work, Margaret Atwood has shifted ground again, and developed stories with a historical interest. She has revisited the history of Ontario during the nineteenth century in *Alias Grace* and in the first half of the twentieth century in *The Blind Assassin*.

Alias Grace (1996)

The real story of Grace Marks, a young woman convicted of murder in Victorian Toronto, had been known to Atwood for many years. She encountered information about Grace in the writings of Susanna Moodie, a nineteenth-century Canadian writer Atwood has turned to throughout her career (note, for instance, her collection of poetry *The Journals of Susanna Moodie*, 1970). Public opinion about Grace's guilt was polarized at the time, with many people decidedly in favour or against her. There were hot arguments in the press, and popular songs were composed on the subject.

Atwood found a great number of archival materials to rely on, even though they contained contradictory explanations of the murder. These documents are quoted at the beginning of each chapter, and they contribute to the powerful historical recreation of this period in Canada. The author has included other texts too, mainly from well-known nineteenth-century writers from Canada, the United Kingdom and the United States: Susanna Moodie, Lord Tennyson, Robert Browning, Christina Rossetti, Emily Dickinson, Edgar Allan Poe, Nathaniel Hawthorne, among many others. High and low materials, literary and non-literary, fictional or not, are placed together in a very postmodern jumble.

Canadian history

The historical background to the personal fate of Grace is extremely rich. Woven into her story are references to the **Rebellions of 1837–38**, which were fresh in the minds of Canadians when the murder took place and may have influenced popular feelings about it. The fact that she was Irish is by no means unimportant. The 1840s were the period of the **Irish Potato Famine**, and Canada was a major destination for the waves of starving immigrants. The hardships Grace experienced in Ireland and during the voyage to North America are surely among the most moving sections in this novel. Atwood is also faithful in her account of the many Irish women who had to turn to domestic

KEY FACTS

Rebellions of 1837–38:
After Canadians unsuccessfully demanded from the British Parliament more participation in their own government, they expressed their dissatisfaction in these two succeeding rebellions. The British authorities appointed Lord Durham to investigate the situation. His famous report pointed out the need for responsible government in the colony.

Irish Potato Famine: The loss of several potato crops in the 1840s caused much starvation and poverty in Ireland, because potatoes constituted the basic fare for most Irish farmers. Many starved to death, while those who could, migrated to North America.

service from their earliest youth in order to survive. Men and women alike, immigrants made an outstanding contribution to the building of the city of Toronto, as *Alias Grace* shows. Moreover, the novel focuses on the relations between three different locations. Canada, where the action is set, must be seen from the perspective of Europe and the United States. Europe does not only mean immigration. It is also the source of political power over the colony (the British Parliament) as well as the source of knowledge and culture. The United States, too, looms large in the novel, since it is steadily acquiring huge economic wealth, fictionally represented by Simon Jordan's family business.

Much of the appeal of this novel lies in the impossibility of ascertaining whether or not Grace Marks did kill her master Thomas Kinnear and the housekeeper Nancy Montgomery, and the probable causes of the murder. Atwood has managed to maintain suspense throughout the narrative and even to the end, which is remarkably open. The tension between differing interpretations of the events is kept by means of the diversity of materials provided in the novel, as well as by the interaction between two characters, one representing subjectivity (Grace Marks) and the other bearing the authority of the objective scientist, Dr. Simon Jordan.

Grace's powerful testimony has the weight of other women's stories, like Offred's in *The Handmaid's Tale*. In her fragmented tale-telling there surface the lives of other humble women used violently and unfairly by men, of their own social class or their betters: her mother, whose body was prematurely aged and ravaged by childbearing and beatings; her friend Mary Whitney, seduced by her young master and killed by an abortion gone wrong; Nancy Montgomery, another unmarried pregnant woman living under the uncertain protection of a well-off man. The blend of stories has a metaphoric equivalent in the quilts Grace is always busy on. Like storytelling, quilt-making involves using disparate materials to create a harmonious whole, just what Grace is doing with the pattern 'the Tree of Paradise' towards the end of the novel:

But three of the triangles in my Tree will be different. One will be
white, from the petticoat I still have that was Mary Whitney's; one
will be faded yellowish, from the prison nightdress I begged as a
keepsake when I left there. And the third will be a pale cotton, a
pink and white floral, cut from the dress of Nancy's that she had
on the first day I was at Mr. Kinnear's, and that I wore on the ferry
to Lewiston, when I was running away.

I will embroider around each one of them with red feather-
stitching, to blend them in as a part of the pattern.

And so we will all be together.

(Alias Grace, ch. 53)

Other women's stories emerge through the character of Simon Jordan:
his mother, a lonely woman who endlessly waits for her son to come
back home and give meaning to her empty life; the young but
unattractive heiress she has chosen for him to marry when he returns,
meant to replenish the family finances and provide an heir; his
landlady, Rachel Humphreys, who lives under a fading pretence of
respectability and the growing fear of poverty.

Simon, a doctor and a scientist, is supposedly the man to bring light
and order to the chaos of lives around him, but his science is unable to
protect him. His name (Simon, like St. Peter, the Christian Apostle)
endows him with the authority of the prophet. However, he falls prey
to the suppressed desires of his body and the uncertainties of his mind.
Scientific discourse proves to be an inappropriate vehicle for the truth
to surface. He eventually retreats in embarrassed failure, and joins the
Union army fighting in the American Civil War. In the end, and this is
one of Atwood's most ironic twists, he loses his memory.

The Blind Assassin (2000)

The Blind Assassin spans another key period of the history of Canada
through the rise and fall of the Chase family. It starts in the late
nineteenth century, when Benjamin Chase established a prosperous
button factory in southern Ontario, and ends in the late twentieth

century, with the transformation of the by then derelict factory into a shopping mall. Similarly, the Chase family mansion, Avilion, has become by the end of the novel an old people's home called Valhalla. Atwood dwells above all on the impact of the two World Wars and the 1930s Depression on the second and third generations as told by the last living Chase and family chronicler, Iris.

The author perceptively emphasizes the contrast between small-town life, represented by the Chase hometown, Port Ticonderoga, and bustling urban centres like Toronto. She also devotes much attention to the sharply different lifestyles of the upper and the lower classes by placing in the shadow of the Chase dynasty another family who serve them and look after them: Reenie's mother, then herself, and still later Reenie's daughter Myra.

Atwood has created here an impressive group of male characters. Benjamin Chase is the self-made man of the late nineteenth century, a builder and an inventor whose social progress is helped by marrying up into an old, respectable but less well-off Montreal family. His three sons, born to wealth and privilege, embody the idealized but naïve principles of a social group that perished in the carnage of the Great War. Edgar and Percival died in battle, and Norval returned a broken man in body and mind. Two new social types rose from the ruins of this war. Richard Griffin is the unprincipled upstart, a rich industrialist that profited from the death of millions in World War I, while Alex is the social rebel that fought for the dignity and survival of the working class during the Depression and that finally vanished without a trace in the ensuing wars in Europe (first the Spanish Civil War of 1936–39 and then World War II, 1939–45).

Women's sufferings

Atwood has revisited some of her major topics in the creation of the women characters. Above all, the need for women to sell out into marriage and respectability reappears here in Grandmother Adelia (Benjamin Chase's wife) and in Iris herself (who similarly brings

Richard Griffin the prestige of old money and position). These two women must sacrifice selves and bodies for dubious results, and they are painfully aware of their loss.

> Every morning I would take a shower, to get rid of the night; to wash off the stuff Richard wore on his hair – some kind of expensive perfumed grease. It rubbed off all over my skin.
>
> Did it bother him that I was indifferent to his nighttime activities, even repelled by them? Not at all. He preferred conquest to cooperation, in every area of life.
>
> Sometimes – increasingly, as time went by – there were bruises, purple, then blue, then yellow. It is remarkable how easily I bruised, said Richard, smiling. A mere touch would do it. He had never known a woman to bruise so easily. It came from being so young and delicate.
>
> He favoured thighs, where it wouldn't show. Anything overt might get in the way of his ambitions.
>
> I sometimes felt as if these marks on my body were a kind of code, which blossomed, then faded, like invisible ink held to a candle. But if they were a code, who held the key to it?
>
> I was sand, I was snow – written on, rewritten, smoothed over.
>
> (*The Blind Assassin*, ch. 9)

Once more in Atwood's fiction, the fearsome consequences of illicit affairs and unwanted pregnancies threaten the lives and peace of mind of women, this time through Laura Chase. She is the most intriguing figure in the novel. The narrator can't let go of her; Laura is her twin and her shadow, the embodiment of the oppression she suffered, the silencing that she had to accept when she married Richard. Laura also represents another common threat for women, since she is repeatedly the target of child abuse within her own household, first by her teacher and later on by her brother-in-law, Richard.

Intertextual playfulness

Like *Alias Grace, The Blind Assassin* is built on a wide range of materials. Interspersed with Iris's narrative are news releases (often from Toronto newspapers like *The Mail and Globe* and *The Star*), letters, and other documents that counterpoint her subjective approach with a supposedly objective view. More importantly, *The Blind Assassin* is two novels rather than only one. It is the title of another narrative that was published under the official authorship of Laura Chase. As Iris tells readers the facts and events in her family's life, her voice is mirrored by another unfolding narrative. Those sections correspond to the secret love affair she had with Alex as well as to the science fiction tale he composed for her during their illicit meetings.

Although the relationship between both stories may not be apparent, since one is more factual and the other more fantastic, they have in common many themes and motifs. In the science fiction tale we find a lively city with striking class differences, where children and women are more likely to suffer and be abused by an inhumane system. Women of the upper classes are used as sacrificial victims, given in marriage with their tongues removed so as to stifle their complaints, and an illegitimate love affair gives two marginal people, the virgin and the assassin, a chance to experience the fulfilment that their society deprives them of.

Yet again, writing is a strategy for survival. Like Offred in *The Handmaid's Tale*, Iris wants to communicate with the future, to tell her suppressed story as well as other women's. A similar need to fictionalize is felt by Alex, the narrator of *The Blind Assassin*, whose science fiction tale creates a much-needed escape from an oppressive reality.

✳ ✳ ✳ *SUMMARY* ✳ ✳ ✳

Atwood's fiction:

- experiments with texts and genres

- plays with voice and perspective

- denounces violence against women

- increasingly blurs the differences between history and fiction.

6 Critical Approaches to Atwood

FEMINIST CRITICISM

Feminist criticism has foregrounded Atwood's sexual politics and her treatment of male and female characters. In particular, the depiction in *The Handmaid's Tale*'s of a **misogynist theocracy** has generated very productive debates on feminist issues, past and present,

such as the relation of women to religion and spirituality, or the differences between generations of feminists.

Women's victimization

Readings of Atwood's writing have at times drawn from the critical ideas she herself laid out in her textbook *Survival* (Anansi, 1972). Starting from the notion that, as a colony, Canada is a collective victim, she defined several patterns for the plots and sentiments of Canadian literature. These patterns she termed 'basic victim positions', and can be used for characters as well as countries:

> Position One: To deny the fact that you are a victim.
> Position Two: To acknowledge the fact that you are a victim, but to explain this as an act of Fate, the Will of God, the dictates of Biology (in the case of women, for instance), the necessity decreed by History, or Economics, or the Unconscious, or any other large general powerful idea.
> Position Three: To acknowledge the fact that you are a victim but to refuse to accept the assumption that the role is inevitable.
> Position Four: To be a creative non-victim.
>
> (*Survival*, ch. 1)

Critics sometimes define the personality of the main female characters and the gender conflict in Atwood's work in terms of these victim positions. These patterns have been applied as well to the work of other contemporary women writers. In her article 'Images of Women's Power in Contemporary Canadian Fiction by Women' (1990), Carol L. Beran examined fiction by Aritha Van Herk and Alice Munro together with *Cat's Eye* and *The Handmaid's Tale* under the light of these victim positions. Beran confirmed that for Atwood, Position Four still remained the ideal her characters strived for many years after the writing of *Survival*.

In *Brutal Choreographies* (University of Massachussetts Press, 1993), J. Brooks Bouson has disclosed many of the key feminist motifs in Atwood's work, such as the examination of images of femininity, the focus on the female body, the power politics of the male gaze, etc. Bouson has most carefully contextualized this fiction by describing its connection with feminist debates of each period, like the pornography issue in relation to *Bodily Harm*.

The handling of the female body in Atwood has been subjected to many interesting approaches, such as Elspeth Cameron's 1985 study of anorexia nervosa in *The Edible Woman*, or Roberta Rubenstein's approach to motherhood in relation to nature and the natural in her 'Nature and Nurture' (1988) essay. Molly Hite's essay 'Writing and Reading the Body' (1988) places Atwood's work together with other women writers, such as Alice Walker, Doris Lessing and Monique Wittig. Using *Lady Oracle* as a case study, Hite explains how Atwood sets out to appropriate the female body and tell the experiences of women as subjects of sexual desire rather than as objects of a male desiring gaze.

Beryl Donaldson Langer has described the sociological features of Atwood's main women characters. She argues that, like Atwood, these women belong to a 'new class' comprising white, middle-class female professionals. They have to confront several contradictions:

... subordination to men of equal or less education; separation from other women by 'cultural capital' and a critical consciousness which renders the taken-for-granted rituals of 'femininity' problematic; and disjunction between the present and the future, created by the absence of viable 'role models' among other women. ('Class and Gender in Margaret Atwood's Fiction' (*Australian–Canadian Studies* 6.1, 1988), p. 91)

Language and identity

Moreover, feminist critics have focused on Atwood's use of language for subverting stable notions of gender and identity, which characterizes all her writing, whether poetry, short stories or longer fiction. In her study '"Yet I Speak, Yet I Exist": Affirmation of the Subject in Atwood's Short Stories', Isabel Carrera has traced the evolution of Atwood's treatment of the subject and its representation in language. In *Dancing Girls*, many stories emphasized the struggle of a female subject against a male antagonist through the opposition she/he. In *Bluebeard's Egg*, however, this polarization gave way to a first-person female narrator who is defining her self in relation to others, mainly with her parents. Finally, in *Wilderness Tips*, there was a collective 'we' built on the changes produced in the individual in a historical context. 'The subject, always complex,' Carrera argues, 'moves from the struggle with itself and the other towards an inclusion of opposites and an extension into its context' (*Margaret Atwood: Writing and Subjectivity* (Macmillan, 1994), p. 243).

How language can be manipulated to serve sexist ends is one of the most striking features of *The Handmaid's Tale*. This phenomenon has been studied by critics such as Michele Lacombe ('The Writing on the Wall', 1986) and Mario Klarer ('The Gender of Orality and Literacy', 1990).

An interesting approach to Atwood's use of language and rhetoric is provided by Nathalie Cooke in 'The Politics of Ventriloquism' (1995). Cooke has analysed the fictive confessions in novels like *The*

Handmaid's Tale and *Cat's Eye*. She has described how Atwood sets up a situation of intimacy where some shameful disclosure is made (for example, the fact that the child Elaine peels the skin off her feet), which leads the listener/reader to feel sympathy for the speaker. Cooke further contends that this form allows Atwood to meet several purposes:

a) lure the reader;
b) implicate the reader in the power politics under discussion;
c) bestow upon him/her the authority and the responsibility of witness. (p. 225)

The study of the confessional form is also the aim of Stephanie Lovelady's 1999 article on *Alias Grace*, as she examines the interplay between the public and the private spheres in the stories of the female characters ('"I Am Telling This to No One But You"'). But that novel involves other languages beyond the merely verbal, as Margaret Rogerson proves in 'Reading the Patchworks in *Alias Grace*' (1998) by looking at quilting as a female language that recurs in the writing of Susan Glaspell and Whitney Otto among other instances.

Gender and genre

The relation between Atwood's attention to gender issues and her handling of diverse genres has also sparkled the critics' interest. Coral Ann Howells believes that for this author 'the main site of conflicting interests lies in inherited fictional forms, and these she insistently analyses and revises' (*Private and Fictional Words* (Methuen, 1987), p. 55). Atwood's remarkable skill to incorporate and at the same time challenge traditional conventions has led Howells to call these novels 'resistant fictions'. For instance, she has explained *Bodily Harm* and *The Handmaid's Tale* as belonging in the **female Gothic** tradition, with their heroines living in hostile environments and being threatened by

KEYWORD

Female Gothic: The idea that there is a distinctive female approach to the use of the Gothic conventions, that can be traced from the eighteenth century to current literature. It was first pointed out by Ellen Moers in *Literary Women* (1978).

manifold dangers. Their survival, however, depends on overcoming the limitations of those stifling stereotypes and on learning to rely on themselves instead of waiting for men to rescue them.

Other interesting deviations from conventional genres have been the subject of several essays. Sybil Korff Vincent has named 'Comic/Gothic' the handling of the Gothic genre by Atwood in *Lady Oracle*, where humour undermines the threats Joan is under. This particular deployment of humour presupposes a female audience ('The Mirror and the Cameo' 1983). Lucy M. Freibert has studied the same novel as a female reassessment of the **picaresque novel**. Her essay describes the episodic structure and plot of *Lady Oracle*, which shuttles to and from several locations, experiences, and relationships, and where the linear progression of the story is frequently interrupted by **flashbacks** ('The Artist as Picaro', 1982).

> ## KEYWORDS
>
> **Picaresque novel:** A kind of fiction in sixteenth-century Spanish literature, focusing on the exploits and adventures of a 'picaro' or rogue who uses all kinds of tricks and cheats in order to survive in a hostile environment.
>
> **Flashback:** An episode that interrupts a narrative following a chronological arrangement by going back to a previous event.

Also, Eleonora Rao has argued that Atwood's fiction is 'located at the interstices of genres and traditions' (*Strategies for Identity*, Peter Lang, 1993, p. xiii), and has traced the powerful intermingling of conventions and modes of writing in Atwood's work of the 1970s and 1980s: the Gothic, science fiction, autobiography, etc. Rao links these features to post-structuralist and postmodernist theories, especially to the decentralization of the subject and to intertextuality.

Women and art

Feminist critics have long emphasized how hard it is for women to gain access to the public sphere of art, and the sacrifices that this often entails. Critics have not missed the fact that many Atwoodian characters are artists, and have read some of her novels as

Künstlerroman or portraits of the artist. Arnold E. and Cathy N. Davidson have considered *Lady Oracle* from the perspective of the politics of writing, in so far as Joan Foster uses literature as an escape from her many problems, and at the same time writes escapist novels for an eager female audience. According to these critics, the novel highlights the evolution of the artist from self-deception to

KEYWORD

Künstlerroman: A novel showcasing the psyche and fate of a young artist. A well-known example is James Joyce's *A Portrait of the Artist As a Young Man* (1916).

enlightenment ('Margaret Atwood's *Lady Oracle*: The Artist as Escapist and Seer', 1978).

For Judith McCombs, Atwood's work of the 1970s displayed female artists who were solitary and hardworking and whose growth was frequently stunted; some were true visionaries while others were sell-outs and manipulators. In both cases, their sexual drive and artistic creativity were closely linked. In the 1980s, however, her artists became middle-aged women with fewer choices ('Atwood's Fictive Portraits of the Artist', 1986).

FEMINIST PSYCHOANALYTIC CRITICISM

Feminist psychoanalytic criticism has drawn attention to the processes of identity formation in Atwood's work, to the split or fragmented personalities of many of her female characters, and to the bonds between mothers and daughters in her novels.

KEYWORD

Feminist psychoanalytic criticism: A kind of literary criticism that uses Freud's and Lacan's theories on the self and the human mind while at the same time revising them from a feminist perspective.

Narcissism

Drawing from French psychoanalysis as well as from American psychiatry, Shannon Hengen has analysed the powerful presence of mirrors in Atwood's writing (*Margaret Atwood's Power*). Mirrors (whether they are objects or other human beings) are instruments in the formation of identity. They give back a reflection that we may accept as ours or not. Jacques Lacan explained that the 'mirror stage' is an important stage in that process. It is the moment when a child is capable of recognizing his/her own image as different from everyone else's. It is a moment of separation and alienation from the mother, who has been the all-powerful figure until then, bringing pleasure and satisfaction of all needs. It also marks the beginning of the child's entry into the social realm, or 'the Symbolic', which includes the acquisition of language.

Narcissism is a personality disorder, a lack of self-esteem that can only be compensated by the perpetual presence of admiring people. This disorder is what Hengen calls 'regressive narcissism', and she explains it is represented in Atwood's work by many male characters: Peter in *The Edible Woman*; David in *Surfacing*; Arthur and his friends in *Lady Oracle*, etc. However, Hengen also defines a 'progressive narcissism' which derives from Julia Kristeva and Luce Irigaray, and that corresponds to the process that allows Atwood's female characters to call themselves Canadian women. This process starts with alienation from themselves due to the influence of men's regressive narcissism. This is why they tend to avoid mirrors until they finally accept the need for identification with other women, which starts with the lost or forgotten mother (or mother figure), that is always a Canadian. Her analysis of this 'progressive narcissism' is particularly enlightening for *Lady Oracle*.

Psychoanalysis and therapy

The interaction between analyst and patient in *Alias Grace* has attracted a number of psychoanalytical readings. Lucie Armitt has pointed out the connections between the pair Simon Jordan–Grace Marks and Sigmund Freud's treatment of Dora in 1900 (*Contemporary Women's Fiction and the Fantastic*, Macmillan, 2000). However, Susan Rowland prefers to discuss the identity of Grace in the light of the theories of Carl Jung ('Imaginal Bodies and Feminine Spirits', 2000).

Mothers and daughters

From the perspective of feminist psychoanalytic criticism, the relationships between mothers and daughters deserve particular attention. These critics seek to display the patterns of identification or rejection of the daughters towards their mothers, and how these processes shape their identity.

This kind of approach has been perceptively used by Barbara Godard in her reading of *Lady Oracle*, when she contends that central to Joan's development is the confrontation with her mother and the realization of how she has contributed to shape Joan's self despite the struggle for a separate identity ('My (m)Other, My Self', 1983).

Other remarkable readings of mother–daughter relationships have been made from the perspectives of myth and religion (see below).

MYTHS, ARCHETYPES AND RELIGION

Atwood's lifelong interest in myths has also appealed to critics in different ways. The spiritual content of her works has been underlined again and again. Feminist theologian Carol P. Christ, for instance, was drawn to the surfacer's quest and the spiritual empowerment of her vision in her 1976 article 'Margaret Atwood: The Surfacing of Woman's Spiritual Quest and Vision'.

Feminist archetypal critic Annis Pratt approached Atwood's novel as an example of women's rebirth narratives in '*Surfacing* and the Rebirth Journey' (*The Art of Margaret Atwood*, Anansi, 1981, 138–57). According to Pratt, the woman hero's quest differs from the male hero's because in order to enact possibilities different from society's restrictive roles, the woman hero must delve into unconscious materials. The world of the unconscious is timeless and spaceless, outside patriarchal norms. Pratt established seven different steps for the rebirth narrative, drawing from the works of many contemporary women writers (Virginia Woolf, Doris Lessing, Marge Piercy, etc.):

1 Leaving the world of the ego: the surfacer drives away from the city.

2 The green world guide helps the hero cross the threshold: the lake becomes the surfacer's door to the unconscious.

3 Confrontation with parental figures.

4 The green world lover: Joe is transformed into a naturistic lover.

5 The shadow: the surfacer's brother represents her violent side.

6 The final descent: the surfacer plunges into the unconscious, or what Pratt terms 'literary insanity'.

7 Ascent and re-entry into society as known: the surfacer is empowered by her quest.

Other feminist archetypal critics have continued to feel the appeal of Atwood's work, and more particularly the impact of her spiritual vision. For instance, in her analysis of Margaret Atwood and Margaret Laurence, *Re/Membering Selves* (Creative, 1996), Coomi Vevaina has adapted the idea of 'survival' to refer not to the body but to the spirit. She describes the different sorts of alienation and identity crisis felt by Atwood's characters and how they are overcome.

Discussions of *Surfacing* have also pointed out the presence of Christian imagery, including the figures of Christ and the Virgin Mary, as Barbara Hill Rigney did in *Lilith's Daughters* (1982). Rigney also remarked on the similarity with the Greek myth of **Demeter and Persephone**, which Sherrill E. Grace has further probed. For Grace, *Surfacing* is a retelling of this 'quintessentially female story' from the perspective of the daughter that successfully searches for the mother ('In Search of Demeter', 1988).

KEY FACT

Demeter and Persephone: Greek myth describing the grief of the earth goddess Demeter (in Latin, Ceres) at the loss of her only daughter Persephone (in Latin, Proserpine), who had been kidnapped by the god of the underworld. While she was grieving nothing grew and no seed sprang up, so eventually an agreement was reached that Persephone would divide her time between her mother and her husband. This myth explains the change of seasons.

Such myths are revized in order to challenge their patriarchal assumptions or handling, as Roberta Sciff-Zamara proved for *Lady Oracle*, a novel that revisions the triple Goddess of mythology, the Great Mother described by the British writer Robert Graves in *The White Goddess* ('The Re/Membering of Female Power in *Lady Oracle*,' 1987).

Religion as a grand narrative that restricts women's lives also features prominently in Atwood's work, most clearly in her theocratic dystopia, *The Handmaid's Tale*. Anna K. Kaler's study of the perversion of religion by the fundamentalist regime of Gilead remains very helpful to understand this aspect of the novel. She points out:

> The obliteration of self into selflessness; the depersonalization of name, clothes, lifestyle; the vows of poverty, chastity, and obedience; the physical disciplines to deny the flesh; even the spiritual journal form itself – all are transmuted from necessary formation devices for women religious into the 'perversions' by which the 'conversions' of the handmaids are effected.
>
> ('"A sister, dipped in blood": Satiric Inversions of the Formation Techniques of Women Religious in Margaret Atwood's *The Handmaid's Tale*', (1989), p. 43)

Yet others have emphasized the non-European components in Atwood's layering of myths. Catherine Sheldrick Ross early on contended that *Surfacing* takes up three kinds of rituals. Christianity offered the possibility of redemption by means of suffering, Americanization was the power to kill, and Indian shamanism was a path to initiation into vision and unity with the world. For Ross, the third one is the only success ('Nancy Drew as Shaman', 1980). Roberta Rubenstein also highlighted how *Surfacing* embraces a reunion with the natural world:

> Having incorporated the redemptive values of the nature deities embodied by her parents' spirits in place of the earlier confusions of distorted Christianity, she has forgiven herself for her sins

against the human condition, thus reaffirming the sacred ties between generations and between man and nature.

> ('*Surfacing*: Margaret Atwood's Journey to the Interior',
> (1976), p. 397)

For Marie Francoise Guédon, the Indian rituals in the novel connect the Euro-American cultures and the Amerindian tradition as well as embodying a doorway into the spiritual realm ('*Surfacing*: Amerindian Myths and Shamanism', 1983). Likewise, Kathryn Van Spanckeren perceived shamanism as a powerful presence in Atwood's works, a device that allows her to transmit a vision that is at the same time female and universal ('Shamanism in the Works of Margaret Atwood', 1988).

CANADIAN NATIONALIST CRITICISM

From the beginning of her career, Atwood became the embodiment of Canadian cultural politics. Many critics have emphasized her role in a Canadian nationalist context, and the way her writings engage the concept of being Canadian. This means, above all, establishing the presence of topics and motifs that can be truly considered 'Canadian', i.e. that can be isolated from the post-colonial influence of the United Kingdom and the neo-colonial impact of the United States.

The wilderness

From the publication of *Surfacing*, critics pointed out the remarkable presence of open, uncultivated natural spaces in Atwood's fiction: the wilderness. The wilderness has been considered a truly Canadian symbol, and one that, according to Coral Ann Howells, 'has multiple functions – as geographical location marker, as spatial metaphor, and as Canada's most popular cultural myth' (*Margaret Atwood* (Macmillan, 1996), p. 21). Although Atwood's later fiction has very often an urban landscape, critics like Howells continue to find in Toronto's ravines the symbolic presence of the wild, as spaces where the miraculous, the transcendental, or the grotesque is more likely to happen.

Ecology: Americans versus Canadians

Atwood's work has been warmly received due to its conservationist concerns. The preoccupation with the land and with humans achieving ecological balance surfaces in many of her writings, such as in *The Handmaid's Tale*, where Gileadeans live in the midst of toxic waste. Critics like Ronald B. Hatch have pointed out Atwood's persistent involvement with conservationism, more openly since the 1980s, when she started participating in campaigns and writing short pieces for green publications. He also relates this involvement with Atwood's changing take on the wilderness, which takes into account Canadians' more urban lifestyles ('Margaret Atwood, the Land, and Ecology', 2000).

A destructive relationship with nature is sometimes embodied by American characters or characters who are identified as American though they may turn out to be Canadians too. *The Handmaid's Tale* is set in Boston. American tourists pollute the lakes and forests of Quebec in *Surfacing*. The contrast between Americans and Canadians as representing two opposing lifestyles and relations to the environment has been the subject of many critical essays, such as Valerie Broege's 1981 article 'Margaret Atwood's Canadians and Americans'.

Canadian History and Politics

Paul Goetsch has recently surveyed Margaret Atwood's Canadian themes in 'Margaret Atwood: A Canadian Nationalist' (2000). Besides the ones described above, he points out two other pervasive topics: the influence of Puritanism on English Canadian attitudes and the national problem of separatism. The former is represented by the difficulties many characters have in leaving behind the restrictive mores of a Puritan upbringing, like Rennie in *Bodily Harm*, who feels stunted by her childhood in Griswold. The latter preoccupation surfaces in many Atwoodian works, such as in the short story 'Polarities'.

POSTCOLONIAL CRITICISM

The past colonization of Canada by Britain and the powerful closeness of the United States has had an impact on all Canadian literature, Atwood's included. Allusions to the inferior status of the colony and to the British influence can be found not only in her historical novels, but also in those with a strong autobiographical turn, like *Cat's Eye*. **Postcolonial criticism** has

KEYWORD

Postcolonial criticism: A kind of criticism that draws attention to how the experience of past or present colonization affects issues of location, language, culture and race in the texts.

suggested similarities between Atwood and authors from other former British colonies: Chinua Achebe in Nigeria, David Malouf and Patrick White in Australia, Witi Ihimaera in New Zealand, and Seamus Heaney in Ireland.

Such links have to do with several issues. For instance, Susan Beckmann indicated how in *Surfacing* the neocolonial power of the United States entailed the loss of language, and therefore, the loss of ancestral connection ('Language as Cultural Identity', 1981). Diana Brydon has perceived intertextual connections between *Surfacing* and Joseph Conrad's *Heart of Darkness*, to the extent that the latter can be considered a 'thematic ancestor' of the former. Both, Brydon argues, encode similar Western anxieties and fear of the wilderness ('"The

KEY FACT

Caliban and Ariel: Two characters in William Shakespeare's *The Tempest* (1611). They are taken by postcolonial critics to embody the personalities of the oppressed and colonized, while the character of Prospero in the same play represents the colonizer and oppressor.

Thematic Ancestor"', 1984). Also interestingly, Roslyn Jolly has traced multiple embodiments of **Caliban and Ariel** in Atwood's *Surfacing* ('Transformations of Caliban and Ariel,' 1986).

Bodily Harm has also been amenable to a postcolonial reading. Set in the Caribbean, it demands that Canadians position themselves in relation to neo-colonial practices. Brydon has charted the move from the voyeuristic mentality of the tourist to the commitment of the reporter in Rennie, a move that is neither smooth nor without ambivalence. For Brydon, the novel's ambiguous end is a refusal to give simple answers to the problems of imperialism and cross-national relations ('Atwood's Postcolonial Imagination', 1995).

POSTMODERNISM

Atwood's fiction has been considered a paradigm of postmodernist self-consciousness. Critics have emphasized several postmodernist traits: metafiction, irony, intertextuality and parody.

Metafiction

In *The Canadian Postmodern* (OUP, 1988), Linda Hutcheon has identified a postmodern paradox in Margaret Atwood's fiction up to *The Handmaid's Tale*. The tension between art as a process (writing, painting, filming, etc.) and art as product (novel, picture, film, etc.) is never resolved. Readers are involved in the creative process necessarily by means of a finished product (the novel itself). Often, this paradox is also conveyed through the conflict between the oral form and the written text, especially in Offred's tale.

Hutcheon has connected Atwood's use of metafiction with her deployment of other arts, especially painting, filming and photography in her fiction. She believes these arts function as metaphors for the written text: 'the stability (and fixity) of the photograph, the (illusory) kinesis of the moving picture, the (deceiving) orality of the tape recording' (*The Canadian Postmodern*, p. 46).

Sharon R. Wilson ('Camera Images', 1987) has defined four main functions for cameras in Atwood's work. First, cameras or photographs may provisionally operate as recorders of experience. Second, they may be used by characters to distance themselves from the object or person photographed. Third, they provide proof of existence, transcending time and at the same time marking the passing of time. Fourth, they focus experience and bring about self-discovery.

Irony

Elsewhere, Hutcheon has pointed out that Atwood's use of **irony** is consistent with other Canadian postmodern literature (*Splitting Images*, OUP, 1991). Because Canadians are uncertain about their identity, she argues, irony becomes a useful tool to articulate their double-voicedness. It is a device that allows them to work within a tradition and at the same time challenge it. Hutcheon perceives this kind of irony at the level of narrative structure in *The Handmaid's Tale*, in how the 'Historical Notes'

KEYWORDS

Irony: In its simplest form, irony involves using words or phrases in such a way that readers should understand the opposite of what they literally mean.

Parody: One work that resembles another, sometimes with a satirical intention.

undercuts Offred's message, introducing a double perspective. She also observes a similar kind of irony in Atwood's use of voice in *Cat's Eye*, where Elaine's middle-aged perspective comments on the attitudes and experiences of her childhood self.

Parody and intertextuality

Martin Kuester has remarked on Atwood's consistent use of **parody**. Her work, he says, provides playful versions of old texts that subvert their meanings and ideological assumptions. Kuester analyses in *Framing Truths* (University of Toronto Press, 1992) how in *Bodily Harm* Rennie recycles and parodies her old travel pieces in a setting that is progressively becoming more oppresive, whereas in *The Handmaid's Tale* Atwood reworks ideas and proposals taken from previous dystopic works, particularly Zamiatin's *We*, Huxley's *Brave New World* and Orwell's *1984*. Hutcheon also perceives a parody of Hawthorne's *The Scarlet Letter* due to the common setting, the use of colour-coding, and the frame narrative.

Many critics have been drawn to the intertextual presence of fairytales in Atwood's work, fiction and poetry alike. Sharon R. Wilson has studied this aspect most comprehensively, pointing out how Atwood, like other contemporary women writers, reworks these traditional tales and transforms their constricting images of men and women. The result of this process is a 'metafairytale', i.e. a literary fragment that is shaped on a fairytale but that calls attention to its fictional status, thus subverting its meaning and ideology. In fact, according to Wilson, Atwood's works are complex metanarratives, involving the revision of one fairytale together with many more, scattered references to other tales, that she terms 'embroidered intertexts'. Wilson describes the intertextual techniques Atwood uses, which range from changing the gender of the fairytale hero, to emphasizing magical transformation as a female experience, or to the use of language to subvert the ideological implications of the tale. She also establishes five main purposes that intertexts serve in Atwood's work:

1   To indicate the quality and nature of her characters' cultural contexts;
2   To signify her characters' entrapment in pre-existing patterns;
3   To comment self-consciously on these patterns;
4   To comment self-consciously on the frame story and other intertexts;
5   To structure the characters' imaginative or 'magical' release from externally imposed patterns, offering the possibility of transformation for the novel's characters, for the country they represent, and for all human beings.

(*Margaret Atwood's Fairy-Tale Sexual Politics*,
UP of Mississippi, 1993, p. 34)

Approaches to Atwood's fiction have come from such a wide range of stylistic and ideological perspectives that it is hard to systematize or transmit their full wealth. The next section includes some suggestions for further work.

✻ ✻ ✻ SUMMARY ✻ ✻ ✻

Critics have attempted to highlight this author's politics as regards:

- feminist thought and the feminist movement of the late twentieth century

- Canadian cultural and national politics, particularly concerning colonial, postcolonial or neocolonial issues

- the practice of postmodern stylistic techniques.

7 Where to Next?

MORE ATWOOD
Check the section on her Major Publications (Chapter 5) and continue reading Atwood's works. You'll find many hours of amusement in her short stories, and food for thought in her poems. Her essays on writing can be a helpful guide for young writers.

Visit Margaret Atwood's homepage, where you will find more biographical data, funny verses, lectures given around the world, and many other intriguing materials:
http://www.web.net/owtoad/

Or visit the official site of The Margaret Atwood Society. There you can access information about Atwood events: what she is writing now, when she is touring, and where. Atwood is an untiring world traveller. Just think: she might be reading at a venue near you very soon!
http://www.cariboo.bc.ca/atwood

CANADIAN CULTURE

Alternatively, Atwood may become your guide into Canadian culture:

* If you are interested in art, find out about a famous artistic movement of the early twentieth century, the Group of Seven, made up of painters such as Tom Tomson. They were fascinated by the landscape of Ontario, that is, by the same kind of wilderness that Atwood depicts in her writing. In fact, many of these landscape paintings become interesting motifs in her fiction. Read her short story 'Death by Landscape', look at the paintings, and compare.

* Learn more about the history of Canada in the twentieth century by reading recent historical fiction: Carol Shields' *The Stone Diaries*, winner of the Pulitzer Prize in 1995, spans the whole twentieth century through a Canadian woman's life story. Anne-Marie MacDonald's *Fall on Your Knees* is a moving family saga set in Cape Breton, while Sky Lee's *Disappearing Moon Cafe* has set hers on the Pacific coast of Canada. Michael Ondaatje's *In the Skin of a Lion* uncloses the participation of immigrants in the building of modern Toronto.

* Compare Atwood's description of the life of poor nineteenth century immigrants like Grace Marks with other accounts. Agnes Sadlier, an Irish woman writer who migrated to Canada and later to the United States in the nineteenth century, wrote about the plight of Irish domestics in her time:
http://www.people.virginia.edu/~eas5e/Sadlier/Intro.html

Like Atwood, contemporary Canadian novelist Jane Urquhart has felt the pathos of the Irish migration to North America around the time of the potato famine, a subject matter that she vividly evokes in *Away*. American writer Andrea Barrett's short story 'Ship Fever' reminds us of the painful conditions these immigrants travelled in, and the even more pitiful reception they encountered upon arrival, in this case at Quebec's Grosse Isle.

WOMEN'S ISSUES

You may want to follow up on some of those women's issues Atwood so often touches on:

* Historically, scientific discourse has contributed to the isolation and marginality of women, as seen in the discussion of *Alias Grace*. A case in point was the famous 'rest cure' imposed on women whose imagination was considered 'too active' for their own good, especially those women who questioned the sanctity of their traditional roles as wives and mothers. The American writer Charlotte Perkins Gilman wrote an account of her own experiences in the heart-gripping short story 'The Yellow Wallpaper'. Read it and find out more about medical cures specifically designed for women's 'troubles'.

* The disease that preoccupied Atwood in *The Edible Woman*, anorexia nervosa, is spreading among young girls in Western countries. The lure of fashion and the high social profile of corpse-thin models bears some of the responsibility for the increase of this self-hating eating disorder. Eavan Boland's poem 'Anorexic' will put you in the skin of an anorexic woman.

* Watch the film version of *The Handmaid's Tale*. Is the situation of women in Gilead so far-fetched? Are there women living in similar situations in our world nowadays? Read other women's dystopias, such as Marge Piercy's *Woman on the Edge of Time*. Learn more about the life of women globally.

Chronology of Major Publications

Novels and poetry by Margaret Atwood can be found all over the world, varying in publisher depending on the country. She regularly publishes with McClelland and Stewart or Anansi in Canada, with Bloomsbury and Virago in the United Kingdom, and with Doubleday and Houghton Mifflin in the US. In the list below, publishers are given only for collections of her criticism, which may be harder to find.

1966	*The Circle Game* (poetry). First major success. Won the Governor General's Award for Poetry 1967.
1968	*The Animals in That Country* poetry).
1969	*The Edible Woman*; first published novel.
1970	*The Journals of Susanna Moodie* poetry) and *Procedures for Underground* (poetry) bring her to the frontline of a new generation of Canadian poets.
1971	*Power Politics* (poetry).
1972	*Surfacing* (novel) is well-received for its stylistic innovations. *Survival: A Thematic Guide to Canadian Literature* (Anansi) raises serious questions about the existence and makeup of a distinctive Canadian Literature. She becomes a prominent figure in Canadian letters.
1974	*You Are Happy* (poetry).
1976	*Lady Oracle* (novel) becomes a best-seller and *Selected Poems* (published in the U.K. as *Poems 1965–1975*) confirms her status as a major Canadian writer.
1977	*Dancing Girls* (short stories) collects stories of women's lives.
1978	*Two-Headed Poems* (poetry).
1979	*Life Before Man* (novel) is not a big success; critics consider it too realistic.
1981	*True Stories* (poetry). With *Bodily Harm* (novel), Atwood returns to the successful formula of the artist narrator.

1982   *Second Words: Selected Critical Prose* (Anansi). She
continues to evaluate the literary tradition of her country.

1983   *Murder in the Dark: Short Fictions and Prose Poems* and
Bluebeard's Egg (short stories). Atwood proves her
masterful use of short prose forms.

1984   *Interlunar* (poetry).

1985   *The Handmaid's Tale*; won the Governor General's Award
for Fiction 1986; shortlisted for the Booker Prize.
International breakthrough. The novel is made into a film
by Director Volker Schlorndorf and released in 1990.

1986   *Selected Poems II: Poems Selected and New, 1976–1986.* A
second comprehensive collection tracing her poetic
accomplishments.

1988   *Cat's Eye* (novel) gets mixed reviews.

1991   *Wilderness Tips* (short stories).

1992   *Good Bones* (short fiction and prose poems). Atwood blurs
the boundaries of different prose forms.

1993   *The Robber Bride* (novel) wins the Commonwealth Writer's
Prize; *Good Bones and Simple Murders* combines previously
published short pieces.

1995   *Morning in the Burned House* (poetry). *Strange Things:
The Malevolent North in Canadian Literature* (Clarendon)
considers the transcending power of several myths in
Canadian Literature.

1996   *Alias Grace* (novel) is acclaimed as a masterpiece.(1998

1998   *Eating Fire: Selected Poems 1965–1995.* The most
comprehensive collection of Atwood's poetry to date.

2000   *The Blind Assassin* (novel) wins the Booker Prize.

2002   *Negotiating with the Dead* (Cambridge UP). Essays on
writing in general and on her career.

GLOSSARY

Anorexia nervosa   An eating disorder, common among adolescents, in which the sufferer gives up eating.

Archetypal criticism   School of literary criticism, prominent in the 1950s and 1960s, which identified the repeated presence of certain myths and archetypes in world literature through the ages. The most representative text is Northrop Frye's *Anatomy of Criticism* (1957).

Bildungsroman   A novel focusing on a character's personal growth, psychological or physical, or both.

Canonical works   Works of art that are considered outstanding and therefore have entered the list of best works in the history of humanity, or 'canon'.

Dystopia   A genre used to examine social issues. Dystopian works describe an imaginary world full of negative features. Usually, the citizens of such worlds live under a tyrannical rule (e.g. George Orwell's *1984*) or in an impersonal, mechanized society (e.g. Aldous Huxley's *Brave New World*) where human life and needs have little worth.

Female Gothic   The idea that there is a distinctive female approach to the use of the Gothic conventions, that can be traced from the eighteenth century to current literature, was first pointed out by Ellen Moers in *Literary Women* (1978).

Feminist psychoanalytic criticism   A kind of literary criticism that uses Freud's and Lacan's theories on the self and the human mind while at the same time revising them from a feminist perspective.

Flashback   An episode that interrupts a narrative following a chronological arrangement by going back to a previous event.

Intertextuality   A characteristic of much postmodern literature. It consists of the insertion of references and allusions to previous texts in another.

Irony   In its simplest form, irony involves using words or phrases in such a way that readers should understand the opposite of what they literally mean.

Künstlerroman A novel showcasing the psyche and fate of a young artist. A well-known example is James Joyce's *A Portrait of the Artist As a Young Man* (1916).

Metafiction Self-conscious fiction. A story that discusses the how and why of writing fiction, and their implications.

Misogynist theocracy A form of government based on religious beliefs, that particularly oppresses women.

Parody One work that resembles another, sometimes with a satirical intention.

Perspectivism The belief that there is no absolute truth. Everything is subjective, the result of each individual perspective.

Picaresque novel A kind of fiction in sixteenth-century Spanish literature, focusing on the exploits and adventures of a 'picaro' or rogue who uses all

kinds of tricks and cheats in order to survive in a hostile environment.

Postcolonial criticism A kind of criticism that draws attention to how the experience of past or present colonization affects issues of location, language, culture and race in the texts.

Postmodernism A literary movement of the second half of the twentieth century, based on the revision of the ideas and aesthetics of modernism. Postmodernism questions the existence of universal truths and distrusts those disciplines that try to provide general answers to the problems of human life, such as History, Religion, or Philosophy.

Quest narrative A narrative form structured around a voyage of discovery. The voyage may be literal or psychological, and the discovery may be of something internal or external to the quester. Generally the quest heals the quester and helps him/her go back home renewed.

Rewriting A technique consisting in telling an old story

from a new, fresh perspective.
Postmodern authors use it in
order to question the ideas and
messages implied in the old texts.
It is also considered a feminist
device, especially since Adrienne
Rich's famous essay 'When We
Dead Awaken' (1976).

Thematic criticism   School of
literary criticism, prominent in
Canada in the 1970s and 1980s,
which discussed the unifying
presence of certain themes in
Canadian literature, especially
those related to the land and
nature.

FURTHER READING

Starting out

Cooke, Nathalie, *Margaret Atwood: A Biography* (Toronto: ECW Press, 1998). An excellent source of information on Atwood, connecting her life and her work. Very lively, a good read.

Howells, Coral Ann, *Margaret Atwood* (London: Macmillan, 1996). Perceptive and comprehensive reading of Atwood's work.

Rao, Eleonora, *Strategies for Identity: The Fiction of Margaret Atwood* (Bern: Peter Lang, 1993). Feminist postmodern approach to the dynamics of gender and genre in Atwood.

Advanced reading

Bouson, J. Brooks, *Brutal Choreographies* (Amherst: The University of Massachusetts Press, 1993). A perceptive feminist reading of Atwood's fiction that pays attention to narrative structure and reader reception.

Davidson, Arnold, and Cathy N. Davidson, eds. *The Art of Margaret Atwood* (Toronto: Anansi, 1981). A classic collection of essays, very useful to trace early critical assessments of Atwood.

Grace, Sherrill, E., and Lorraine Weir, eds. *Margaret Atwood: Language, Text, and System* (Vancouver: University of British Columbia Press, 1983). Another classic collection of essays, mostly from a structuralist approach.

Hengen, Shannon, *Margaret Atwood's Power* (Toronto: Second Story Press, 1993). An innovative approach to Atwood's career, psychoanalytic in perspective.

Howells, Coral Ann, *Private and Fictional Words* (London: Methuen, 1987). Insightful analysis placing Atwood in the context of other Canadian women novelists.

Hutcheon, Linda, *The Canadian Postmodern* (Toronto: Oxford UP, 1988). Excellent for placing Atwood in her cultural and national ambience – see also title below.

Hutcheon, Linda, *Splitting Images: Contemporary Canadian Ironies* (Toronto: Oxford UP, 1991).

Kuester, Martin, *Framing Truths: Parodic Structures in Contemporary English–Canadian Historical Novels* (Toronto: University of Toronto Press, 1992). A postmodern reading of several Canadian authors, including Atwood.

Lacroix, Jean-Michel, Jacques Leclaire, et Jack Warwick, eds. *The Handmaid's Tale, Roman Protéen* (Rouen: Publications de l'Université de Rouen, 1999). Includes a lecture by Atwood on the genesis of her most popular novel, and a round table where she answers frequently asked questions on it, besides critical essays (one in French).

McCombs, Judith, ed. *Critical Essays on Margaret Atwood* (Boston: Hall, 1988). Another classic collection of essays on Atwood, several of them outstanding.

Mendez-Egle, Beatrice, ed. *Margaret Atwood: Reflection and Reality* (Edinburgh: Pan American University, 1987). This collection contains many enlightening essays on Atwood.

Nicholson, Colin, ed. *Margaret Atwood: Writing and Subjectivity* (London: Macmillan, 1994). A remarkable collection of essays covering a wide range of works by Atwood.

Nischik, Reingard M., ed. *Margaret Atwood: Works and Impact* (NY: Candem House, 2000). A well-documented and very comprehensive approach to Atwood's career.

Staels, Hilde, *Margaret Atwood's Novels: A Study of Narrative Discourse* (Tuebingen: Francke Verlag, 1995). Provides analysis of literary form in Atwood's novels up to *The Robber Bride*.

Van Spanckeren, Kathryn, and Jan Garden Castro, eds. *Margaret Atwood: Vision and Forms* (Carbondale: Southern Illinois UP, 1988). Many essays in this collection are must-reads.

Vevaina, Coomi S., *Re/Membering Selves* (New Delhi: Creative, 1996). Compares the spiritual visions of Atwood and fellow-Canadian writer Margaret Laurence.

Wilson, Sharon R., *Margaret Atwood's Fairy-Tale Sexual Politics* (Jackson: UP of Mississippi, 1993). Very comprehensive reading of the fairytales in Atwood's fiction and poetry, connecting them to the visual arts.

York, Lorraine M., ed. *Various Atwoods* (Toronto: Anansi, 1993). Another interesting collection, containing both vintage criticism and new takes on Atwood.

INDEX